GROWING POINTS IN THEOLOGY

EXODUS AND SINAI IN
HISTORY AND TRADITION

Exodus and Sinai in History and Tradition

E. W. NICHOLSON

Fellow and Dean of Pembroke College, Cambridge

John Knox Press
Richmond, Virginia

British edition published by
Basil Blackwell, Oxford

American edition published by
John Knox Press, Richmond, Virginia

Library of Congress Cataloging in Publication Data
Nicholson, Ernest Wilson
Exodus and Sinai in history and tradition
(Growing points in theology series)
Bibliography: p.
1. Exodus, The. 2. Sinai, Mount. 3. Bible. O.T. Pentateuch—Criticism, interpretation, etc. 4. Jews—History—To entrance into Canaan. I. Title.
BS 680.E9N52 1973 222'.1'066 73-6595
ISBN 0-8042-0200-1

Printed in Great Britain

To
Rosalind and Kathryn
Peter and Jane

Preface

I am indebted to various colleagues for much help and advice in the preparation of this book and especially to Professor George Anderson, Professor John Emerton and Dr. Ronald Clements. Not for the first time I am also indebted to Mr. Henry Schollick and I record my gratitude to him for including this book in the series Growing Points in Theology and for his generous co-operation in publishing it.

Pembroke College, Cambridge   Ernest W. Nicholson
Lent 1973

Abbreviations

ATANT	Abhandlungen zur Theologie des Alten und Neuen Testaments
BA	*The Biblical Archaeologist*
BASOR	Bulletin of the American Schools of Oriental Research
BWANT	Beiträge zur Wissenschaft vom Alten und Neuen Testament
BZAW	Beihefte zur Zeitschrift für die alttestamentliche Wissenschaft
EvTh	*Evangelische Theologie*
FRLANT	Forschungen zur Religion und Literatur des Alten und Neuen Testaments
HAT	Handbuch zum Alten Testament
JBL	*Journal of Biblical Literature*
LXX	The Septuagint
MT	The Masoretic Text
OTS	*Oudtestamentische Studiën*
SEÅ	*Svensk Exegetisk Årsbok*
StTh	*Studia Theologica*
SVT	Supplements to Vetus Testamentum
TvT	*Tijdschrift voor Theologie*
ÜG	M. Noth, *Überlieferungsgeschichte des Pentateuch*, Stuttgart 1948
VT	*Vetus Testamentum*
WMANT	Wissenschaftliche Monographien zum Alten und Neuen Testament
ZAW	*Zeitschrift für die alttestamentliche Wissenschaft*

Contents

Preface   vii

Abbreviations   ix

Introduction   xiii

1 The Separation of Exodus and Sinai in History and Tradition   1

2 Exodus, Covenant and Treaty   33

3 Observations, Suggestions and Conclusions   53

Bibliography   85

Indices   91

Introduction

Reduced to its barest outlines, the biblical narrative of the origins and early history of Israel as presented in the Hexateuch records that the twelve tribes of Israel, which were the descendants of the twelve sons of Jacob and through him of Abraham and Isaac, having been enslaved in Egypt escaped under the leadership of Moses and journeyed to mount Sinai where they entered solemnly into covenant with Yahweh to whom they attributed their miraculous deliverance from bondage. Subsequently they remained in the wilderness for forty years and finally entered the promised land of Canaan. This straightforward account of Israel's origins and early history forms the backbone of the Hexateuch and is presented wholly or partly or is at least presupposed by the various documents (J, E, D, P) which the Hexateuch comprises.

This history of Israel as presented in the Hexateuch contains five major themes as follows: (1) the promise to the patriarchs; (2) the Exodus from Egypt; (3) the theophany and covenant at mount Sinai; (4) the wandering in the wilderness; and (5) the entry into the land of Canaan. As we now have them they are the final deposit of a long process of theological reflection and development as well as literary activity, ranging from their presentation in the earliest Pentateuchal document J (widely agreed to have been composed in the period of the united monarchy) to their latest presentation by the author of P in the post-exilic period. Literary analysis has revealed that they were already fused together and presented in elaborate form in J. It is clear, however, that these themes and their respective traditions had already undergone a long process of development before being taken up by the author of J in the relatively late period in which he worked, a period several centuries removed from the events which he narrates. Accordingly, a great deal of research has been carried out during the past generation into the pre-literary stage in the development of these traditions and the interweaving of their respective themes. In other words, scholars have sought to determine how and in what circumstances and by what means these traditions originated and were developed and fused together in early Israel. Together with this has gone the discussion of what we can say of the historical events to which these traditions witness or which they presuppose.

In this book we shall be concerned with only one of the many problems to which this investigation of the Pentateuchal traditions and the historical events behind them has given rise. But it is a crucial problem and certainly one of the most controversial in current Pentateuchal research, for it can scarcely be questioned that the Exodus from Egypt and the making of the covenant at Sinai are of central importance in the Old Testament's presentation and understanding of Israel's faith. In the Pentateuch the two complexes of tradition concerning the Exodus and the covenant at Sinai are fused together and the narrative draws a direct historical connection between the Exodus and Sinai events. But this relationship between the Exodus and Sinai traditions and the events to which they witness has been questioned and it has been argued by a number of scholars that the events were historically unrelated to one another and that the traditions to which they gave rise were transmitted independently of one another and combined only at a relatively late stage in Israel's history and the development of her faith.

This separation of the events and traditions of Exodus and Sinai has not gone unchallenged. On the contrary it has been vigorously contested and the historical connection between the events as well as the close interrelationship of their respective traditions in Israel's life from the beginning have been defended and reaffirmed by many scholars.

It is with the discussion which has centred on this problem that we are concerned in this study. The first chapter comprises a *résumé* of the more important recent works in which the separation of the events and traditions of Exodus and Sinai has been advocated, together with various criticisms which have been or may be levelled against such a view. In the second chapter I turn to a brief discussion of the main arguments advanced recently in favour of an original historical relationship between these events and the interrelationship of their respective traditions from the beginning.

With regard to these first two chapters, it need hardly be said that numerous contributions have been made to this debate. It has not been my intention, however, to discuss every one of them. What I have attempted to do is to describe the main trends in the debate and to outline the major arguments adduced for and against the separation of the events and traditions of the Exodus and Sinai. Finally, in the third chapter I have made a number of observations and advanced some suggestions which I believe to be justified in the present state of our knowledge and which I hope will take the discussion of this complex problem a stage further and provoke fresh discussion of it.

I

The Separation of Exodus and Sinai in History and Tradition

During the past generation the most influential works in which it has been argued that the Exodus and Sinai traditions and the events behind them were originally unrelated to one another have come from the German scholars G. von Rad and M. Noth. Von Rad's major work in this connection (*Das formgeschichtliche Problem des Hexateuch*),[1] a study which more than any other constitutes the basis of the current discussion of the problem, appeared in 1938, thus antedating Noth's work on the Pentateuchal traditions which was published in 1948 and which with regard to this problem presupposes von Rad's conclusions.[2] In what follows we shall summarize the work of these two scholars and mention briefly some other contributions which advocate a similar point of view. Subsequently we shall turn to the various criticisms which may be levelled against the views advanced by them.

I

G. von Rad: Israel's Creed

In his famous work 'The Form-Critical Problem of the Hexateuch' von Rad seeks to deal with the question of the basic structure of

[1] References here are to 'The Form-Critical Problem of the Hexateuch', in *The Problem of the Hexateuch and other Essays*, E.T. by E. W. Trueman Dicken, Edinburgh and London 1966, 1–78.

[2] M. Noth, *Überlieferungsgeschichte des Pentateuch*, Stuttgart 1948 (hereafter abbreviated *ÜG*). Cf. also his *The History of Israel*, E.T. revised by P. R. Ackroyd, London 1960, to which we shall also be referring frequently below.

BES

the Hexateuch as we now have it. He begins with and indeed
makes the basis of his investigation the passage in Deuteronomy
26:5b–9 which he describes as a short historical creed:

> My father was a wandering Aramaean who went down into
> Egypt and dwelt there, few in number; and there he became
> a great, numerous and populous nation. And the Egyptians
> treated us harshly, and afflicted us and imposed upon us cruel
> slavery. Then we cried to Yahweh the God of our fathers, and
> Yahweh heard our cry, and saw our affliction, our toil, and
> our oppression; and Yahweh brought us out of Egypt with a
> strong hand and an outstretched arm, with great terror, and
> with signs and wonders; and he brought us into this place and
> gave us this land, a land flowing with milk and honey.

Von Rad acknowledges that this short passage contains some
Deuteronomic phrases. But when allowance has been made for a
certain amount of editing by those who placed it in its present
context, this passage, in his opinion, is very much older than the
book of Deuteronomy in which it is now found. It is, he argues, an
ancient confession of faith which centres on a recitation of Yahweh's saving deeds on Israel's behalf which were fundamental in
the faith of the community of Israel. In reciting this confession the
worshipper fully identified himself with the community and indeed
in so doing became its mouthpiece.

Von Rad classifies this passage as a creed; it has, he believes, all
the characteristics of a creed and indeed probably represents the
earliest example of Israel's creed. Furthermore, if it is a creed there
must have been a specific cultic occasion on which it was recited,
and von Rad believes that such an occasion can be identified.
Before turning to a consideration of this, however, he draws our
attention to one striking feature of this old creed, that is, the
complete absence of any reference to the Sinai covenant. It begins
with the patriarch Jacob (he is the 'wandering Aramaean' referred
to; Abraham and Isaac came in at a later stage in the development
of the Patriarchal traditions)[3] and proceeds through the captivity
of his descendants in Egypt, the Exodus from bondage, and the
entry into the promised land of Canaan without any reference to
the making of the covenant on mount Sinai which immediately
follows the Exodus in the Pentateuch as we now have it.

In order to show that this absence of any reference to the Sinai

[3] Von Rad attributes this development to the Yahwist (cf. op. cit., 54ff.).

covenant in Deuteronomy 26:5b–9 is not unique, von Rad cites other texts which outline the *Heilsgeschichte* and which likewise omit any reference to it. One such passage is Deuteronomy 6:20ff. The summary of the salvation history here presented, which is very similar to that in Deuteronomy 26:5b–9, is all the more striking for its silence concerning the Sinai events, von Rad argues, since the very question asked is concerned precisely with what Israel believed to have been announced to her at Sinai: 'What is the meaning of the precepts and the statutes and the laws which Yahweh our God has commanded you?.' According to von Rad the form was already 'so rigidly fixed that even in this instance, where they might seem quite essential, these [Sinai] events could find no place'.[4]

Yet another text cited in this connection is Joshua 24:2b–13. This is a much more expansive account of the *Heilsgeschichte*, supplying, unlike the two passages in Deuteronomy, many details concerning the events narrated (the miracle at the Reed Sea, Balaam, the war with the inhabitants of Jericho, etc.). Here again, however, the covenant at Sinai is not mentioned and this is all the more striking in view of the details supplied in recalling the other events: 'The revelation of Yahweh and the sealing of the covenant were, after all', von Rad points out, 'events of such epoch-making significance that they could certainly have been brought in along-side the story of Balaam or the mention of the hornet if their inclusion had been regarded as in any way relevant. But the basic pattern seems to have known nothing of these things; and we are thus faced with the remarkable fact that this *genre* allowed for the interpolation of small details, but not for so fundamental an alteration as would have been occasioned by the introduction of the events of mount Sinai.'[5]

Von Rad concludes that the three passages referred to were all compiled according to the same plan, which was a canonical pattern of the *Heilsgeschichte* long since fixed as to its main essentials, a fact which is evidenced by the consistent omission of any mention of the covenant at Sinai. On the basis of this he suggests that such a recital of the main elements of the *Heils-geschichte* 'must have been an invariable feature of the ancient Israelite cult, either as a straightforward credal statement or as a hortatory address to the congregation'.[6]

---

[4] Ibid., 6.   [5] Ibid., 7f.   [6] Ibid., 8.

By way of further support for the main conclusions thus arrived at, von Rad draws attention to a number of what he describes as free adaptations of the creed in cult-lyrics elsewhere in the Old Testament which likewise contain no reference to the making of the covenant at Sinai (Exod. 6.15; 1 Sam. 12; Pss. 78, 105, 135, 136), and then finally to the passage in Nehemiah 9:6ff. where at last the Sinai events are mentioned along with the other events of the *Heilsgeschichte*. But this passage, he argues, represents a late stage when the older, fixed canonical form had fallen apart, since, in addition to the Sinai events, the passage also includes the creation and dwells on the monarchical period right down to the post- exilic period itself, all of which was never part of the older credal schema.[7]

On the basis of these conclusions von Rad argues that the Sinai events gave rise to a tradition of their own, a tradition which had its own history in early Israel and which remained quite separate from the canonical pattern of the saving history, the *Landnahme* (settlement) tradition as he terms it, contained in the creed in Deuteronomy 26:5b–9 and other similar texts. Similarly the *Landnahme* tradition also had its own separate history.

But this immediately gives rise to an important question, for while the Sinai events do not find any place in the recitation of the *Heilsgeschichte* as presented in the credal formulations they certainly have a place within the narrative of the Pentateuch as a whole where they are described as having followed the Exodus from Egypt. The question arises, therefore, whether the Pentateuchal presentation of the Sinai events as following those of the Exodus renders untenable the conclusions arrived at concerning the separation of the two sets of tradition in the summaries of the saving history in the credal formulations.

That it does not is argued by von Rad who appeals in this connection to a long established view concerning the Pentateuchal narrative of the events which followed the Exodus. Since Wellhausen many scholars have maintained that behind the present J narrative in the book of Exodus lies a form of the story in which the Israelites after crossing the Reed Sea moved on immediately not to Sinai but to Kadesh. The evidence for this is briefly as follows.[8]

---

[7] Ibid., 8ff.
[8] Cf. J. Wellhausen, *Prolegomena to the History of Israel*, E.T. by J. S. Black and A. Menzies, Edinburgh 1885, 342ff., 439; H. Gressmann, *Mose und seine Zeit. Ein Kommentar zu den Mose-Sagen*, FRLANT 18 (Göttingen 1913), 123ff.

Exodus 15:22 records that when the Israelites had crossed the Reed Sea they journeyed three days into the wilderness without water. The name of the place at which they arrived is not mentioned, but it was probably Kadesh, for they came then (*v.* 23) to Marah where they found 'bitter' water which was sweetened by Moses (*v.* 25) after the people had 'murmured' against him (*v.* 24). It is then recorded (*v.* 25) that Yahweh[9] 'made for them a statute and a law and there he put them to the test'. This, it is maintained, would seem to refer to the 'testing' at Massah (cf. Exod. 17:1–7). But Massah is identified with Meribah (Exod. 17:7) which itself is located at Kadesh (cf. Num. 20:13; 27:14; Deut. 32:51).[10] On the basis of these considerations it is therefore argued that these traditions gathered originally around Kadesh and its associated springs. It seems therefore, it is argued, that there were originally two separate accounts of what happened after the Israelites had escaped from Egypt which have subsequently been combined. Accordingly, scholars have distinguished between a cycle of Kadesh narratives in Exodus 17–18, Numbers 10–14, and a Sinai cycle in Exodus 19–24, 32–4 (JE). It is only the former, it is then maintained, which is closely united with the Exodus narratives; the Sinai narratives have only subsequently been superimposed upon the Exodus-Kadesh narratives. Hence, von Rad concludes, the Pentateuchal narrative does not contradict the findings from his examination of the creeds that the Sinai tradition was originally quite separate from the Exodus-settlement tradition. His form-critical investigation substantiates the same conclusion arrived at by earlier scholars on different grounds.

In the Sinai pericope in Exodus 19–24 the theophany and the making of the covenant are the dominant elements which, von Rad argues, 'from the point of view of both content and structure . . . form a fixed and complete cycle of tradition'.[11] Furthermore, as a corollary to his findings from the examination of the creeds, he points out that the Sinai pericope affords no place to the redemptive acts of God in the Exodus and wanderings. He is therefore able to conclude: 'In each case we are dealing with material of

[9] MT reads 'he' but clearly it refers to Yahweh.

[10] On Exod. 17:6f. where it might seem that Massah and Meribah are associated with Horeb see M. Noth, *Exodus*, E.T. by J. S. Bowden, London 1962, 140, where it is argued that the detail 'at Horeb' is a subsequent addition. On Massah and Meribah in Exod. 17:1–7, see below 27, n. 73.

[11] Op. cit., 18.

quite a different kind. The exodus tradition bears witness to the redemptive purpose of God revealed to Israel in its travels from Egypt to Canaan; it is a "redemptive history". The Sinai tradition testifies to the divine justice, revealed to the nation and made binding upon it: it is apodeictic law.' This, he further argues, is substantiated by a number of passages which represent variants of the Sinai tradition similar to the adaptations of the old credal formulation to which he has already drawn attention (e.g. Deut. 33:2, 4; Judg. 5:4f.; Hab. 3:3ff.).

Having thus argued for this original independence of the Sinai tradition from the settlement tradition, von Rad proceeds to a closer examination of the nature of them both and of their respective settings in life in early Israel. His investigation and conclusions may be briefly summarized as follows.

A. THE SINAI TRADITION

An examination of the Pentateuchal narrative of the events at Sinai reveals that the three literary strands which it now comprises (J, E, P) share a basic schema which is fixed in its essential elements. When the Israelites arrive at mount Sinai they are ritually purified and prepared for the theophany of Yahweh on the third day. On the third day they experience the manifestation of Yahweh amidst fire, smoke, and the blast of the trumpet. Moses then receives the law from Yahweh and proclaims it to the people who are bound under oath to observe it, after which the covenant is ratified with a sacrifice.[12]

Von Rad argues that what we are dealing with in this tradition which underlies the Pentateuchal narrative of the Sinai events is not a literary record of the historical course of events but a sacral tradition which had its original home within a cultic setting. That is to say, in its nature and structure as well as in the individual elements which it comprises, it points for its *Sitz im Leben* to a recurring liturgical act, a festival in early Israel.

At this point von Rad cites with approval the conclusions already arrived at by S. Mowinckel in his book *Le Décalogue*[13] where it is argued that the origin and basis of the Sinai covenant story is to be

---

[12] So E. Von Rad assigns the record of the covenant meal in Exod. 24:9ff. to J.

[13] S. Mowinckel, *Le Décalogue*, Paris 1927, 114ff.

traced to a cultic ceremony in Jerusalem. The major difference in this connection between von Rad and Mowinckel is that the former traces the origins of the festival in question to the pre-monarchical period in Israel's history.

Von Rad thus argues that a clearly discernible cultic schema underlies the Sinai pericope in Exodus 19–24:[14]

(i)   presentation of the events at Sinai (19);
(ii)   the reading of the law (20:1–23:19);
(iii)   promise of blessing (23:20ff.);
(iv)   ratification of the covenant (24:1–11).

It is then concluded that such a cultic schema points for its origin to a recurring cultic occasion in early Israel which took the form of a festival of covenant renewal. Where and when did such a festival take place?

On the basis of Deuteronomy 31:10–11, von Rad maintains that such a festival was celebrated at the feast of Tabernacles in the autumn;[15] he leaves open the question whether it took place annually or, as this same text suggests, once every seven years. As to the origin and early history of this festival, following Sellin and Noth,[16] he points to a number of texts in the Old Testament which preserve the tradition of the proclamation of the divine law within a cultic ceremony at the old sanctuary at Shechem. Noth in particular had argued that Joshua 24 preserves the memory of the formation of the twelve-tribe federation or amphictyony of early Israel, but had also argued that the occasion described had not been a once and for all event but a periodically repeated ceremony of covenant renewal.[17] In fact, on the basis of Joshua 24 as well as other texts such as Deuteronomy 27, which preserves the memory of an early proclamation of the commandments to the community on what was clearly a cultic occasion, von Rad finds that the festival at Shechem followed precisely the same pattern which he believes to underly the Sinai pericope.[18]

Von Rad therefore concludes that the Sinai covenant tradition

---

[14] Op. cit., 27. Von Rad discerns the same schema underlying the book of Deut. (cf. ibid., 26ff.) as well as texts such as Pss. 50, 81.

[15] Exod. 19:1 (P) which might point to the feast of Weeks as the occasion for such a festival is regarded as reflecting later practice (op. cit., 34ff.).

[16] E. Sellin, *Geschichte des israelitische-jüdischen Volkes*, I, 2nd ed., Leipzig 1935, 101; M. Noth, *Das System der zwölf Stämme Israels*, BWANT IV:1, Stuttgart 1930 (hereafter abbreviated *Das System*), 140ff.

[17] See below, 13f.   [18] G. von Rad, op. cit., 38.

in early, pre-monarchical Israel was a sacral tradition which had its *Sitz im Leben* in a cultic festival which was celebrated periodically at the ancient sanctuary at Shechem at the autumn feast of Tabernacles. Furthermore, this cultic festival afforded no place within its structure and contents to the settlement tradition as presented in the old credal formulation in Deuteronomy 26:5b–9 and elsewhere in the Old Testament. This gives rise to the question of the nature and *Sitz im Leben* of this settlement tradition.

B. THE SETTLEMENT TRADITION

Von Rad classifies this tradition too as a cultic tradition. That is, like the Sinai tradition, it also points for its setting in life to a recurring liturgical occasion in the life of early Israel, a festival which centred on celebrating Yahweh's redemptive acts on Israel's behalf in history culminating in the gift of the promised land to Israel (hence von Rad's definition of this tradition as the *Landnahme* tradition). The cultic *Sitz im Leben* of the settlement tradition is evidenced by Deuteronomy 26:5b–9 which von Rad believes to be the earliest version of the credal recitation of the saving history. For Deuteronomy 26 relates the recitation of this creed to the presentation of the 'first-fruits'. It is true that here the act of presenting the first-fruits and reciting the creed is described as being performed by the individual worshipper. But this is a secondary element in the tradition, possibly first introduced by the Deuteronomic authors. In the earlier period it was not a personal affair 'but expressly an undertaking of the whole community', that is, an act of public and corporate worship.[19]

In relating the recitation of the creed to the offering of the first-fruits, Deuteronomy 26 provides the clue to when the ceremony in question took place, for the calendars in the Old Testament all include provision for a cultic festival which included the presentation of the produce of the earth, the feast of Weeks in early summer referred to in Numbers 28:26 specifically as 'the day of the first-fruits' and in Exodus 23:16 as 'the harvest festival of the first-fruits which you have made'. Leviticus 23:17 indicates that it was the fruit of the land presented in the form of wheaten loaves which was offered at this festival. It is accordingly argued that the offering of agricultural produce envisaged by Deuteronomy 26 corresponds

[19] G. von Rad, op. cit., 42.

to that of Exodus 23:13, 34:12 and Leviticus 23:17; the ceremony
in question was therefore observed at the feast of Weeks. Von Rad
thus concludes:[20]

> The creed as we have it in Deuteronomy xxvi 5ff. is the
> cult-legend[21] of the Feast of Weeks—that is, it contains those
> elements of Yahwistic faith which were celebrated at the Feast
> of Weeks. . . . The Feast of Weeks was originally, of course,
> a non-Israelite harvest festival. The cult-legend provided
> the historical justification which enabled Israel to adopt as
> its own the ancient Canaanite festival, and from the stand-
> point of the old Yahwistic faith, it offered quite the handiest
> method of appropriating an agricultural festival. By the use
> of the creed, the congregation acknowledges the redemptive
> sovereignty of Yahweh, now seen as the giver of the cultivable
> land.

Where in early Israel (for the tradition and the festival are
certainly of ancient origin, von Rad argues) did this feast of Weeks
which centred on the celebration of Yahweh's redemptive acts take
place? In determining this he directs our attention to the old
tradition, found for the most part in the book of Joshua, which
centres on the sanctuary of Gilgal in the Jordan valley near
Jericho. According to the traditions underlying Joshua 3–4,
Israel after crossing the Jordan went to Gilgal where a sanctuary
was established and the people circumcised. In addition, Gilgal
was also the location of the 'camp' from which the tribes went out
on their conquering exploits and to which they returned subsequently (Josh. 9:16; 10:6, 9, 15). Most significant of all, however,
is the record that it was at Gilgal that Joshua made the apportion-
ment of the promised land to the tribes (Josh. 14:6–14; 18:2–10).[22]
When these considerations concerning Gilgal are taken in con-
junction with the conclusion arrived at above that the settlement
tradition as summarized in the old creed in Deuteronomy 26: 5b–9
was the cult-legend of the feast of Weeks in early Israel and
celebrated above all *the gift of the land*, then it is plausible to

---

[20] Ibid., 38.

[21] By 'legend' von Rad means of course that which was 'read out'
(*legenda*) at such a festival.

[22] According to von Rad we should read Gilgal and not Shiloh in Josh.
18:9, 10.

conclude, von Rad maintains, that it was precisely at the old sanctuary at Gilgal that that festival was celebrated.

There were thus, according to von Rad, two major cultic festivals in early Israel each of which had its own particular nature and form. The feast of Tabernacles as it was celebrated at Shechem was the *Sitz im Leben* of the Sinai covenant tradition, whilst the settlement tradition had its home at Gilgal where it was celebrated annually on the occasion of the feast of Weeks in early summer. Both sets of tradition, Sinai and *Landnahme*, remained quite separate and were brought together, it is argued, only at a relatively late date. It was the Yahwist, von Rad maintains, who first joined them in writing his epic, probably sometime during the united monarchy under David and Solomon. The basis for the Yahwist's work was the creed which embodied the themes of the call of the patriarch Jacob, the Exodus, the wandering in the wilderness and the entry into the promised land. Into this schema the Yahwist inserted the Sinai tradition. At the same time he expanded the patriarchal tradition to include Abraham and Isaac and prefaced the whole with an account of the primaeval history in Genesis 1–11.

Von Rad has little to say of the actual historical events behind the Exodus and Sinai traditions; he is concerned more with the history of the traditions to which they each gave rise or were a part. Elsewhere, however, he states that the events of Exodus and Sinai were themselves originally unrelated: 'It is more likely that traditions belonging to different groups were united with one another at a later date'.[23]

A number of questions immediately arise concerning von Rad's work. Of primary importance is whether Deuteronomy 26:5b–9 is as ancient as he believes or whether it is quite simply a late Deuteronomic formulation. Furthermore, are the contents of these so-called creeds as 'fixed' as is suggested by him? Is it really clear that the occasion presupposed by Deuteronomy 26 is the feast of Weeks? Can Exodus 15:22–18:27 be regarded as a Kadesh cycle of stories, as von Rad following older critics believes? With these and other questions we shall concern ourselves presently. At this stage, however, we must turn to the important work of Noth. We shall see that with regard to the separation of the Exodus and Sinai traditions Noth closely follows von Rad. Since, however,

[23] Cf. G. von Rad, *Old Testament Theology*, I, E.T. by D. M. Stalker, Edinburgh and London 1962, 8.

other aspects of his work on the Pentateuchal traditions as a whole as well as his views on the origins and constitution of early Israel, have exercised great influence on the ongoing discussion of the problem with which we are concerned, we must familiarize ourselves with them.

II

M. Noth: Tribes and Traditions in early Israel

In order to understand Noth's views on the problem in hand it is necessary to know his theory of the origins and early history of Israel, since his views on the latter are to a very considerable degree presupposed in his discussion of the origins and history of the Pentateuchal traditions and the means whereby they were woven together to form the Pentateuchal narrative. In what follows, therefore, we shall first of all outline briefly his work on early Israelite history after which we shall turn to his study of the history of the Pentateuchal traditions with particular reference to those of Exodus and Sinai.

A. According to Noth, Israel, properly understood, originated and assumed its classic form as a sacral union or confederacy of twelve tribes on the soil of Canaan in the pre-monarchical period. This tribal league came into existence only after numerous separate clans and groups of clans of semi-nomads had made their entry into the land at one time or another and were there gradually bound together into the separate tribes which eventually together constituted Israel.[24] It is therefore impossible, according to Noth, to investigate the history of Israel before the settlement since by definition there was no Israel before the emergence of the twelve-tribe league in Canaan. All that we can say of the period before this is that there were disparate semi-nomadic clans and groups of clans each of which led its own separate existence and maintained its own traditions. He argues that the separate tribes of Israel did not exist as such before the settlement since most of them assumed the tribal form in which we encounter them in the Old Testament only after the settlement. That is to say, the tribes which went to make up Israel came into existence for the most part as the result

[24] M. Noth, *Das System*, 75ff.; *The History of Israel*, 68ff.

of the consolidation of originally separate clans which after they
had entered the land occupied a common region or area there.[25]

The actual settlement of the clans and their formation into
tribes was a protracted process and can be reconstructed only in
very general terms.[26] On the basis of a number of observations,
especially concerning ancient traditions about the tribes and
concerning collections of old aphorisms relating to them such as
are contained in Genesis 49, Noth concludes that the first to have
settled were the tribes Reuben, Simeon, Levi, Judah, Issachar and
Zebulun, which are grouped together in the earliest traditions and
referred to as 'the sons of Leah'. It was at a later time that the
clans which constituted the tribes of Benjamin came in, to be
followed subsequently by 'the house of Joseph'. Joseph and
Benjamin are referred to in the Old Testament as 'the sons of
Rachel' and Noth suggests that the historical basis of this relationship was brought about by the proximity of these tribes to one
another in central Palestine[27] and also possibly because Benjamin
was connected in some way, of which we no longer have any
information, with the settlement of Joseph.[28] As for the other
tribes, the so-called concubine tribes, Asher, Dan, Naphtali and
Gad, Noth in his earlier work believed them to have made their
entry and to have settled in the land sometime after the settlement
of the Leah group and before the advent of Joseph,[29] though in
his later work he related the coming of Gad to the same migration
as Joseph.[30]

For Noth one of the most important features in the traditions
concerning early Israel is the constancy of the figure twelve as the
number of the tribes; in spite of changes in the fortunes of the
tribes—Levi, most notably, seems to have ceased to be a 'secular'
tribe at an early stage—this number is maintained. This constancy
in the number of the tribes is accounted for by Noth in his well-
known thesis that early Israel took the form of a tribal league on the
analogy of the city-state confederations later attested in Greece and

[25] Thus, for example, the tribe of Judah is believed by Noth to have
originated in the consolidation of clans which settled in the region of
Canaan known as 'the mount of Judah' from which they then acquired
their name. A similar process is posited for other tribes.

[26] Cf. M. Noth, *The History of Israel*, 64–84.

[27] The Benjaminites are believed by Noth (ibid., 63) to have received
their name as 'southerners' because of their geographical position *vis-à-vis*
Joseph further north.

[28] Cf. *Das System*, 82f.   [29] Ibid., 83ff.   [30] *The History of Israel*, 75.

Italy and known to the Greeks as amphictyonies. Thus early Israel in both its external constitution and its institutions was, Noth maintains, a twelve-tribe amphictyony.[31]

Of the institutions of this Israelite amphictyony, the most prominent was, as in the later European leagues, the central sanctuary the oversight and upkeep of which was the responsibility of each tribe for one month of the year. In Israel the Ark was the common cultic object of the tribes and the various sanctuaries in which it was located from time to time were each in turn the central sanctuaries of Israel. According to Noth, Shechem was the first of these central shrines and was succeeded by Bethel then Gilgal and finally Shiloh. It was primarily their communal worship of Yahweh at the central sanctuary which formed the focal point and binding factor in the life of the Israelite confederation. We can no longer ascertain the precise form of the amphictyonic cultic observances, but there is some evidence that the most important cultic occasion was an annual festival at which each of the tribes was officially represented and which appears to have centred mainly on a confession of faith in Yahweh together with a proclamation of the divine law and a covenant-making ceremony. This much Noth ascertains from the narrative in Joshua 24 which very probably, he believes, reflects a regularly recurring cultic event in early Israel.[32] Indeed, according to Noth, it was this proclamation of the divine law which constituted the distinctive character of Israel's worship as it was the authority of this law in the ordering of tribal life which marked Israel off from the surrounding peoples.[33] It is especially in connection with this proclamation of divine law that the office of 'judge' (cf. Judg. 10:1–5; 12:7–15) is to be understood.[34]

As to the origin of the twelve-tribe amphictyony of early Israel, Noth finds evidence of this in Joshua 24. Scholars before him had already drawn attention to the importance and antiquity of the material in this chapter and it had been pointed out that the

[31] For Noth's discussion of this see *Das System*, 61ff.; *The History of Israel*, 87ff.

[32] For Noth's discussion of this chapter see *Das System*, 66ff., 133ff.; *Josua* HAT 7 (Tübingen 1953), in loc.

[33] On this see especially Noth's work, 'The Laws in the Pentateuch: Their Assumptions and Meaning', in *The Laws in the Pentateuch and Other Essays*, E.T. by D. R. Ap-Thomas, Edinburgh and London 1966, 1–107.

[34] Cf. *The History of Israel*, 101.

occasion described seems to presuppose the presence at Shechem of two separate groups. On the one hand there was Joshua and his 'house' and on the other those who were called upon to 'put away the gods' which their fathers had worshipped beyond the Euphrates (Josh. 24:14–15). Noth suggests that it was under the leadership of the house of Joseph, represented by Joshua, that the twelve-tribe amphictyony was formed at Shechem, and that the basis of this twelve-tribe league was the earlier six-tribe league constituted by the Leah tribes, whose centre also appears originally to have been Shechem (cf. Gen. 34). Noth also conjectures that this earlier six-tribe amphictyony—he believes that the number of these Leah tribes indicates that they constituted an amphictyony—may have been the original bearer of the name Israel.[35] Thus it is maintained that after the entry into Canaan of the house of Joseph, Joshua gathered all twelve tribes, that is, their representatives, at Shechem where they entered into a covenant with Yahweh and henceforth became known as Israel. Properly speaking, the name Israel designates this twelve-tribe amphictyony; its later use to connote the Northern Kingdom as against the southern state of Judah is secondary.

B. Noth finds five main 'themes' running through the Pentateuch: the promise to the patriarchs, the Exodus from Egypt, the wandering in the wilderness, the revelation at Sinai, and the entry into the land of Canaan.[36] These themes have their basis in five distinct traditions. However, both their all-Israelite connotation and their interrelationship in the Pentateuch narrative as it lies before us is a secondary development. As traditions relating to the pre-settlement period they cannot originally have been concerned with Israel which did not come into existence until after the disparate clans had made their separate entry into Canaan and were there eventually united into tribes and subsequently brought together to constitute Israel. These traditions and the events behind them would have been originally unrelated to each other as separate traditions and events belonging to and experienced by

[35] The suggestion that the Leah group was called Israel was made in *Das System*, 83ff. but is not repeated in *The History of Israel*. On the Leah tribes see further *Das System*, 75ff.

[36] Noth's discussion of these themes and their underlying traditions is presented in *ÜG*, 45–67. Cf. also his *The History of Israel*, 109–37.

originally separate and independent clans or groups of clans.[37] Hence in this connection Noth points with approval to von Rad's form-critical study which isolates the Sinai tradition from the traditions referred to in the historical creed. Noth is also concerned, however, to trace the pre-history of the credal traditions which were also, he believes, originally quite unrelated and independent traditions behind which lie separate and unconnected events.

The origins of these traditions and the means whereby they were given their all-Israelite orientation and were woven together are, as understood by Noth, very much bound up with the origins, formation and communal life of the twelve-tribe league of Israel. Of cardinal importance in the process was the central sanctuary of the confederation, for it would have been especially at the amphictyonic cultic festivals at which all the tribes were represented that originally local traditions would have become the common property, so to speak, of all the tribes and would thus have acquired an all-Israelite orientation. In this way there emerged, Noth believes, an all-Israelite complex of sagas describing the origins of Israel and narrating the stirring events which called her into being and gave her her identity as the people of Yahweh. This complex would not have been composed by an individual 'author' or indeed by a series of 'authors', but would have emerged gradually through successive stages of development at the hands of 'story tellers' (*Erzählern*), 'bards', on the occasions when the tribes and clans assembled for cultic worship.[38] Noth believes that this complex of sagas, which he designates G (= *Grundlage*), became the basis of the work of both the Yahwist and the Elohist at a later time and accounts for the close parallels in both structure and contents between the J and E documents.[39] The history of the combination of the individual traditions to form this Pentateuchal *Grundlage* as reconstructed by Noth is briefly as follows.

The crystallization point of the Pentateuch narrative as a whole was the confession that Yahweh brought Israel forth from the land of Egypt: 'In the "bringing forth from Israel" we have the original confession of Israel—formulated in more or less hymnic form—and at the same time the nucleus of the entire, expansive, later Pentateuch tradition'.[40] The Exodus tradition, Noth maintains, was from the beginning an all-Israelite tradition. That is, it did not

[37] Cf. *ÜG*, 45ff., 48ff.   [38] Ibid., 47.   [39] Ibid., 40ff.   [40] Ibid., 52.

originally belong, like the other main themes of the Pentateuch
(except the Sinai tradition) to one particular tribe or group of
tribes subsequently to be appropriated by other tribes in the
Israelite amphictyony. It existed from the very earliest times in
hymnic form and is found in such form in numerous different
contexts throughout the Old Testament. Furthermore, so significant and important was the Exodus for Israel that it is impossible
to limit such hymnic confessions of the Exodus to any particular
Sitz im Leben in Israel's cultic calendar. According to Noth, it was
the 'miracle at the sea' which was the act that was first and chiefly
meant when Israel confessed that it was 'Yahweh who led us up
out of Egypt'.[41] He states: 'From this point of view all the previous
acts of God against the Egyptians seem like a prelude which cul-
minates in the decisive event at the sea. In this way then the
narrative of the deliverance at the sea is to be regarded as the real
nucleus of the exodus theme, and in the present tradition it forms
not only the end but also the goal and climax of the whole. . . .'[42]

How then did the deliverance from bondage in Egypt in which
the miracle at the sea was the decisive act become an all-Israelite
tradition? For, historically speaking, the events themselves—Noth
believes that there is enough evidence to date them in the thirteenth century B.C.[43]—cannot have been the experience of Israel
which did not emerge as an historical reality until later and whose
ancestors did not share a common history before they were united
into the tribes of Israel in the promised land. He rejects any
suggestion that the central Palestinian tribes Joseph and Benjamin
were those which had been in Egypt, as has sometimes been
argued. The dominant part played by these tribes in the Pentateuch
narrative of the bondage has no historical basis but arose because
the tradition as we now have it was moulded very largely by these
tribes.[44] This in turn arose because the house of Joseph had not
only been predominantly responsible for the actual formation of
the twelve-tribe amphictyony of Israel but also continued, together with its neighbour Benjamin, to play a dominant role in the
life of the tribal league, as is evidenced for example by the fact that
the central sanctuaries of the amphictyony were all located in the
territory of these two tribes. Noth's own solution to the problem
is that those who had been in Egypt and had experienced the
deliverance from bondage and the miracle at the sea did not

[41] Cf. *ÜG*, 52f.; *Exodus*, 104.   [42] *Exodus*, 104f.
[43] M. Noth, *The History of Israel*, 118f.   [44] Ibid., 116ff.

constitute one particular tribe of Israel; nor were they absorbed into a particular group of tribes within Israel. Rather they were absorbed throughout the tribes as a whole. He suggests that those who had migrated to Egypt had previously been connected in some manner with nomadic shepherds who lived on the borders of Palestine and with whom in the course of time they were to form the tribes of Israel. After their flight from Egypt those who had been enslaved journeyed back to this territory on the borders of Palestine bringing with them the news of their marvellous deliverance from the Egyptians which so moved those with whom they met again that they passed the story on everywhere and transmitted it to their descendants as though it had happened to them all. 'In this way', Noth concludes, 'the confession of faith in the God who had manifested himself so gloriously by delivering them from the hand of the Egyptians became the common property of the whole of Israel and one of the foundations of the faith which lived in the institution of the sacred confederacy of the twelve tribes under the protection of the binding law of God.'[45]

Finally, Noth asserts that besides being formulated in hymnic style this confession would have been elaborated into an extended narrative at the hands of story-tellers on occasions of assemblies for worship throughout the territory of the twelve tribes. In addition to the destruction of the Egyptians at the sea, which formed the climax of the narration, this narrative would also have contained a description of the sojourn of the Israelites in Egypt, their subjection to forced labour, the plagues visited upon the Egyptians— the plague narratives arose as a secondary expansion of the Passover narrative, the ancient Passover rite having been associated with the Exodus tradition at a very early stage[46]—and their eventual escape. Noth believes that the Exodus narrative was the first stage in the emergence of G.[47]

According to Noth, the development of the Exodus tradition was followed by the development and inclusion of the theme of the entry into the land of Canaan. To the combination of these first two themes were subsequently added those of the promise to the patriarchs and the wandering in the wilderness.

Following the evidence adduced by von Rad from Israel's historical creed, as presented in its oldest formulation in Deuteronomy 26:5b–9, Noth believes that the Sinai covenant tradition was the last major theme of the Pentateuch to be combined with

---

[45] *The History of Israel*, 118.   [46] *ÜG*, 70ff.   [47] Ibid., 54.

the others.[48] He rejects von Rad's view, however, that its incorporation was the work of the Yahwist and argues instead that it was already united with the other themes in the pre-monarchical period to form the original Pentateuch narrative G.

From an historical point of view, the origins and basis of the Sinai traditions are difficult to discern. Noth accepts the widely held view that Yahweh belongs originally to Sinai (cf. Deut. 33:2; Judg. 5:4f.; Hab. 3:3ff.) and was worshipped there by semi-nomadic clans who lived in its vicinity or made pilgrimages to it. He suggests that the decisive revelation of Yahweh, which formed the basis of the Sinai tradition, may have taken place in the course of a pilgrimage to the holy mountain by such clans. At a later time the descendants of these Yahweh-worshipping clans were among those who came together in the land of Canaan to form the tribes of Israel, bringing the worship of Yahweh with them and the memory of their momentous experience of his awful manifestation to them on Sinai. Subsequently, after the formation of the Israelite amphictyony at Shechem, the Sinai tradition was handed down within the context of the all-Israelite covenant renewal festival. By this means the Sinai tradition acquired an all-Israelite orientation at the earliest period in the history of the tribal league. Furthermore, the *Sitz im Leben* in which it was transmitted gave rise to a significant development of this tradition, for it so dominated the covenant festival that the covenant between Yahweh and Israel which was inaugurated at Shechem was transferred back to Sinai itself.

As to the relationship between the events of Exodus and Sinai, Noth believes that, just as there was no original connection between the separate traditions to which these events gave rise, so also there was probably no connection between the events themselves.[49] They were experienced by quite separate groups and the traditions concerning them were united only after the descendants of these groups had been absorbed and united in the tribes of Israel. According to Noth, the clans which were the bearers of the Sinai tradition were amongst the earliest to settle in the land and unite to form some of the tribes later to constitute Israel. This means that they belonged to the Leah tribes whose entry into Canaan antedated that of the other tribes.[50] This in turn means that Israel's worship of Yahweh derived from these Leah tribes. When,

---

[48] *ÜG*, 62f.   [49] *The History of Israel*, 132.
[50] *ÜG*, 65f.; *The History of Israel*, 136, n. 2.

after the formation of the Leah group, other clans which had experienced the miraculous deliverance from Egypt entered the land, the conviction grew that the God who had so marvellously delivered them from the Egyptians was none other than Yahweh the God of Sinai.[51]

Why was it that a tradition of such fundamental importance for Israel as the Sinai tradition did not find a place in the Pentateuch narrative until the final stages of the development of that narrative? Whilst only conjectures are possible here, Noth believes the reason to be historical. He states: 'The deliverance from Egypt which took place "by the sea" was so much to the fore in the Israelite tradition, as far as it is known to us, as the precondition of the occupation of the land, that one gets the impression that, as the divine action on which the very existence of Israel was based, it was a more lively and immediate memory than the divine appearance on Sinai, which was only transmitted within the framework of a regular religious observance.'[52]

Finally, as to the question under the influence of which tribes the Sinai tradition was included in the Pentateuch narrative G, the fact that it was from the beginning an all-Israelite tradition raises the possibility that any tribe could have been responsible. Nevertheless, in view of the fact that the southern tribes, according to Noth, appear to have influenced the later stages in the development of G,[53] he believes that it was they also who were largely responsible for the inclusion of the Sinai covenant tradition.

Several important issues arise from Noth's work. His suggestion that an original Pentateuchal narrative G lies behind the work of both the Yahwist and the Elohist is compelling. At the same time recent research has more and more questioned this theory of an early Israelite amphictyony,[54] which is of such obvious importance for the way in which he believes G to have developed. Again, his view that the original basis of the Sinai tradition was the theophany is noteworthy. If it can be substantiated, however, is he correct in maintaining that it was associated at an early stage with the covenant in the context of a covenant festival? When did

[51] *The History of Israel*, 136f.

[52] *The History of Israel*, 132. Cf. *ÜG*, 65f.

[53] Noth argues (*ÜG*, 61f.) that they were responsible for the development of the patriarchal tradition so as to include Abraham and Isaac, and were directly responsible for the development and inclusion of the theme of the wandering in the wilderness in G.

[54] Cf. 27, n. 75.

the covenant between Israel and Yahweh or the belief in such a covenant arise? Can his conclusion that there was no connection between the events of Exodus and Sinai be sustained? We shall be concerned with these and other questions at a later stage in our study. At this stage we must turn to a critical examination of von Rad's work which is also of fundamental importance for and is presupposed by Noth's own thesis.

III

We have seen that according to von Rad the so-called historical creed in Deuteronomy 26:5b–9, though worked over to some extent by the Deuteronomic authors who placed it in its present context, is a formulation of great antiquity and very probably the oldest example of Israel's creed we possess. However, a careful examination of this passage with regard both to its vocabulary and to its style reveals that, far from being a 'working over' (*Übermalung*) of an old formulation, it more probably owes its composition as a whole to the Deuteronomic authors themselves.[55] The repetitious character of the Deuteronomic paraenetic style is immediately apparent: 'a *great, numerous and populous* nation' (*v.* 5); 'the Egyptians *treated us harshly, and afflicted us, and imposed upon us cruel slavery*' (*v.* 6); 'and Yahweh *heard our cry, and saw our affliction, our toil, and our oppression*' (*v.* 7); 'and Yahweh brought us out of Egypt *with a strong hand and an outstretched arm, with great terror, and with signs and wonders*' (*v.* 8). We observe also the following

---

[55] For a textual study of the passage see C. H. W. Brekelmans, 'Het "historische Credo" van Israël', *TvT* 3 (1963), 1–11; L. Rost, 'Das kleine geschichtliche Credo', in *Das kleine Credo und andere Studien zum Alten Testament*, Heidelberg 1965, 11–25; W. Richter, 'Beobachtungen zur theologischen Systembildung in der alt. Literatur anhand des "kleinen geschichtlichen Credo"' in *Wahrheit und Verkündigung*, Festschrift for M. Schmaus, Paderborn 1967, 191–5; J. P. Hyatt, 'Were there an Ancient Historical Credo in Israel and an Independent Sinai Tradition?' in *Translating and Understanding the Old Testament* (Essays in Honor of H. G. May), ed. by H. Thomas Frank and W. L. Reed, New York–Nashville 1970, 152–70; N. Lohfink, 'Zum "kleinen geschichtlichen Credo" Dtn. 26, 5–9', *Theologie und Philosophie* 46 (1971), 19–39. These scholars all agree that the passage is either entirely or for the most part a late composition and either entirely or substantially the work of the Deuteronomic authors. Rost and Lohfink believe that an ancient nucleus can be isolated from *vv.* 5 and 10a.

words and expressions found either only in the Deuteronomic literature or very characteristic of it: 'few in number' (Deut. 26:5; 28:62);[56] 'the God of our (your, their) fathers', found in a few passages elsewhere in the Old Testament but very frequently in Deuteronomy (Deut. 1:11, 21; 4:1; 6:3; 21:1; 26:7; 27:3; 29:24. Cf. also Josh. 18:3; Judg. 2:21); 'with a mighty hand and an outstretched arm' occurs mainly in the Deuteronomic corpus (Deut. 4:34; 5:15; 7:19; 11:2; 1 Kgs. 8:42. Cf. also Deut. 9:29; 2 Kgs. 17:36), and in Deuteronomic passages in Jeremiah (Jer. 21:5; 32:21. Cf. also 27:5; 32:17), twice in Ezekiel (Ezek. 20:33, 34. Deuteronomic influence?), and once in the late Psalm 136; 'with great terror' only in Deuteronomy 4:34; 34:12 and in the Deuteronomic passage Jeremiah 32:21; 'with signs and wonders' is found seldom elsewhere but very frequently in Deuteronomy (Deut. 4:34; 6:22; 7:19; 13:2, 3; 26:8; 28:46; 29:2; 34:11); 'a land flowing with milk and honey', though occurring elsewhere, is frequent in Deuteronomy (Deut. 6:3; 11:9; 26:9, 15; 27:3; 31:20. Cf. Josh. 5:6) and in Deuteronomic passages in Jeremiah (Jer. 11:5 32:22), and in Ezekiel 20:6, 15 (Deuteronomic influence?). Some of the remaining terminology was possibly derived from the JE narrative of the Exodus tradition in the Pentateuch.[57]

From a literary point of view there is little reason to doubt that Deuteronomy 26:5b–9 owes its composition to the Deuteronomic authors and is thus a late formulation summarizing the saving events of Israel's history and probably already presupposing the JE narrative in the Pentateuch.[58] Furthermore, its meaning and purpose are also readily understood within the context of the Deuteronomic theology. V. 10a, which cannot, contrary to von

[56] Lohfink (op. cit., 28) adjudges this 'undeuteronomisch' on the grounds that Deut. 28:62 is a late Deuteronomic passage dependent for its usage of this expression on 26:5. Even if this is so, however, the fact remains that it does occur in the latter passage and nowhere else in the Old Testament outside Deut. This being so it seems strange to say that it is not Deuteronomic. For it must be borne in mind that the passage with which we are dealing is in the book of Deut. and the onus is surely upon those who believe the passage to have been composed, whether wholly or partly, by others to show that it and its component parts were not composed by the authors of the book in which it occurs.

[57] Cf. C. H. W. Brekelmans, op. cit., p. 4 n. 12; L. Rost, op. cit., 12ff.

[58] Richter (op. cit.) in particular argues forcibly that the passage presupposes J and E. Cf. also B. S. Childs, 'Deuteronomic Formulae of the Exodus Traditions', in *Hebräische Wortforschung*, Festschrift for W. Baumgartner, SVT 16 (Leiden 1967), 39.

Rad's opinion, be separated from *vv.* 5b–9,[59] forms the climax to
the confession and provides the explanation of its recital and the
accompanying presentation of the first-fruits: the purpose of both
the confession and the dedication is to affirm that it is Yahweh who
has given the land to his people whom he has redeemed and that
it is he alone who bestows upon them all the blessings which it
affords, the blessings of a 'land flowing with milk and honey'. That
the land and its fertility and produce are Yahweh's gracious gift
to Israel for which her thanks and faithfulness are demanded is a
theme found throughout Deuteronomy (cf. Deut. 6:10ff.; 7:12ff.;
8:7ff., 11ff.; 11:10ff., 13ff.; etc.). Furthermore, we are hardly
mistaken in seeing in Deuteronomy 26:5b–10 a further example of
the anti-Canaanite polemic which pervades the book as a whole
and a denial that it was Baal who was responsible for the fertility
and produce of the land, a denial which resounds vehemently
through the book of Hosea (cf. esp. Hos. 2), with which in this,
as in other respects, Deuteronomy has long been recognized to
have close affinities. A further consideration in favour of such an
interpretation of Deuteronomy 26:5b–10 as an acknowledgment
that it is Yahweh who bestows the land and its produce upon
Israel is as follows. According to the introduction of this confession, the worshipper is required to present an offering 'of the first of
all the fruit of the land' (Deut. 26:2). We may ask whether such an
expression can, as von Rad argues, refer only to the feast of Weeks
or whether, as the above interpretation suggests, Israel is here
being called upon to acknowledge that *all* the good of the land is
the gift of Yahweh.[60] In this respect Vriezen has compared the
confession in Deuteronomy 26:5b–10 with the offering formula in
1 Chronicles 29:10ff.: 'for all things come of thee and of thy own
have we given thee' (*v.* 14). Vriezen concludes: 'In principle I see
no difference between this offering-formula (Deut. 26:5b–10) and
the one which David pronounces in 1 Chronicles 29:10ff. when he
presents all the treasures involved in the building of the Temple,
although Yahweh is here pictured as the Lord of all things, while

---

[59] The verse begins with the concluding *weʿatāh* 'and now' and *v.* 10b
provides the continuation of the description of the act. To separate it
from what precedes is unwarranted. Cf. C. H. W. Brekelmans, op. cit., 8;
T. C. Vriezen, 'The Credo in the Old Testament', in *Die ou Testamentiese
Wergemeenskop in Suid Afrika: Studies in the Psalms*, ed. by A. H. van
Zyl, Potchefstroom 1963, 14.

[60] Cf. A. S. van der Woude, *Uittocht en Sinaï*, Nijkerk 1961, 86. See
further below, 32.

in Deuteronomy he is the Lord of Israel, who has given all things to Israel.'[61]

How then are we to explain the absence of any reference to Sinai in Deuteronomy 26:5b–10? It obviously cannot be due to any rigorous separation between the Exodus and Sinai traditions such as von Rad proposes, for no such separation can be detected in the Deuteronomic presentation of these traditions; for the authors of Deuteronomy both the traditions and the events behind them are interrelated and historically connected. A perfectly acceptable explanation has been advanced by Weiser as follows.[62] Deuteronomy 26:5b–10 and similar passages are concerned with recalling briefly the redemptive acts wrought by Yahweh *on Israel's behalf* and culminating in the giving of the land. But the event of Sinai, he points out, is not an event in the same sense as the historical events of the Exodus and the settlement. The Sinai event, as it is presented to us in the Old Testament, was rather *the encounter between Yahweh and his people*, an encounter which centred on the proclamation of the will of Yahweh and the acceptance of the commandments by the people whom he had redeemed. To this we may make the following additional observation. If the interpretation of Deuteronomy 26:5b–10 outlined above is accepted, then in affirming Yahweh's Lordship the worshipper in performing the liturgy laid down in this passage was surely *ipso facto* affirming the basic demand of the covenant as Deuteronomy presents it. In support of this we recall that elsewhere in Deuteronomy the gift of the land and Israel's continued possession of it and the benefits which it brings to her are dependent precisely upon her obedience to the will of Yahweh expressed in terms of faithfulness to the law (cf. Deut. 6:10ff.; 7:12ff.; 8:11ff.; 11:10ff.). In other words, the recitation of the *Heilsgeschichte* in Deuteronomy 26:5b–10 leads up to and is bound up with the allegiance Israel is to give Yahweh to whom she owes everything; the very issue at stake here, as the Deuteronomic authors see it, is precisely the acknowledgment of Yahweh as Lord of Israel, an acknowledgment which is of the very essence of the covenant theology in Deuteronomy.

We turn now to a brief consideration of Deuteronomy 6:21–23, which von Rad cites as a further example of Israel's creed in which

---

[61] T. C. Vriezen, op. cit., 14.

[62] A. Weiser, *Introduction to the Old Testament*, E.T. by D. M. Barton, London 1961, 86.

there is no mention of Sinai. And here the result is even clearer than in the case of 26:5b–10. Von Rad would of course separate *vv.* 21–3 from their context. But such a separation is inadmissible, for *vv.* 20–5 constitute a unit which displays what is perhaps best described as a catechetical form as follows:

(*a*) the question: 'What is the meaning of the testimonies and the statutes and the ordinances which Yahweh our God has commanded you?', then you shall say to your son:

(*b*) answer and explanation: 'We were Pharaoh's slaves in Egypt; and Yahweh brought us out of Egypt with a mighty hand; and Yahweh wrought signs and wonders, great and grievous, against Egypt, against Pharaoh and all his household, before our eyes; and he brought us out from there, that he might bring us in and give us the land which he swore to our fathers.'

(*c*) restatement of the practice which prompted the question: 'So Yahweh commanded us to do all these statutes, to fear Yahweh our God, for our good always, that he might preserve us alive, as at this day. And it will be righteousness for us, if we are careful to do all this commandment before Yahweh our God, as he has commanded us.'

The entire passage, including *vv.* 21–3, is thoroughly Deuteronomic in both style and vocabulary; the creed certainly cannot be isolated from or regarded as an old formulation inserted into its present context. And here obviously the Exodus-settlement tradition is inseparably linked with the Sinai-covenant tradition: the Deuteronomic authors here recall Yahweh's redemptive acts on Israel's behalf as precisely the basis on which obedience to the covenant stipulations is demanded. The mention of the Sinai event in the so-called creed itself would have been quite out of place, since of course obedience to the covenant laws is precisely the question at issue.

The third main text in the Old Testament which von Rad cites as evidence of the original independence of the credal themes from the Sinai tradition is Joshua 24:2–13 where again the *Heilsgeschichte* is recited without any reference to the Sinai event. The literary history of this chapter is of considerable complexity. Many scholars believe that it comprises an ancient nucleus which has been worked over to a greater or lesser extent by the Deuteronomic authors.[63] though the view that it is entirely a Deuter-

[63] Cf. M. Noth, *Josua*, 135ff. D. J. McCarthy, *Treaty and Covenant*, Rome 1963, 145ff., 171f., holds that the Deuteronomic reworking was

onomic composition has also been advanced.[64] Its present structure
is complex and McCarthy has shown that it is not possible to find
in it, as a number of scholars have concluded, the full covenant
form.[65] Nevertheless, it is possible to conclude, he maintains, that
Joshua 24 'is a complete sermon built up out of the elements which
do appear in the covenant tradition'.[66] And for our present purposes
the significance of this is that it is accordingly impossible to separate, as does von Rad, the recitation of the *Heilsgeschichte* in *vv.*
2–13 from the demand to serve Yahweh which follows in *vv.* 14ff.
The recitation of the saving acts of Yahweh in this chapter is,
together with other admonitions and warnings in the same chapter,
the very basis upon which fidelity to the covenant is demanded.
The so-called creed in Joshua 24 thus serves the same function as
in Deuteronomy 6:20ff.

Arising from these passages in Deuteronomy and Joshua it
appears that a major weakness in von Rad's theory is the belief
that the recitation of the saving history was an end in itself. Vriezen
raises the question whether a creed such as that proposed by von
Rad is to be expected in ancient Israel and remarks:[67] 'It is typical
of Israel (on this score Jewish theology is right), that it, in contrast
to the Christian church, never had a definite, directly circum-
scribed, generally valid, "canonical" confession of faith. Therefore, the question comes to the fore: Does the idea of a credo not
import something that is foreign to the world of ancient Israel?
Israel is hardly concerned with a battle round a confession, but
with the service of Yahweh and the adherence to His law. Torah
and cult are at stake.' Furthermore, we may observe, by way of
further support for Vriezen's opinion, that contrary to von Rad's
contention the so-called creed is not rigidly limited with regard to
the historical events to which it may allude.[68] It seems rather that

---

nothing more than 'a few touches added to the older material' (ibid., 171,
n. 6) and would regard *vv.* 19–24, contrary to Noth, as belonging to the
original material (ibid., 150, n. 14). None the less, McCarthy argues that
the passage as a whole is substantially a unity and rejects any attempt to
separate the verses comprising the historical recital from the ensuing
verses centring on the covenant theme.

[64] E.g., H. G. May, 'Joshua', in *Peake's Commentary*, 2nd ed. by H. H.
Rowley and M. Black, London and Edinburgh 1962, 303.
[65] D. J. McCarthy, op. cit., 145ff.   [66] Ibid., 148.
[67] T. C. Vriezen, op. cit., 12.
[68] For this observation see A. S. van der Woude, op. cit., 9.

the content of the *Heilsgeschichte* depends upon the particular
juncture in Israel's history in which the Old Testament records
that it was recited. Thus Exodus 19:3b–8 mentions only the
Exodus and the journey to Sinai;[69] the texts in Deuteronomy go
up to the settlement, as also does Joshua 24; 1 Samuel 12 includes the period of the Judges,[70] whilst Nehemiah 9 proceeds up
to the time of Ezra-Nehemiah. The fact is that wherever the
recitation occurs it is related to a specific purpose and function. It
remains true that in most texts the Sinai event is not mentioned
among the saving events of Israel's history, but we may repeat
Weiser's observation noted earlier: the event of Sinai is not an event
in the same sense as the historical events of the Exodus and the
settlement, events in which Yahweh acted *on behalf of Israel*; the
Sinai event concerns God's *encounter with his people*.

Finally, we must consider briefly the argument cited by von Rad
in favour of his conclusions from the Pentateuchal narrative as a
whole, that is, the well known view of Wellhausen and others who
maintained that the Sinai story has been superimposed upon an
earlier Exodus-Kadesh narrative still discernible behind J. Can
this older point of view be sustained?

In fact, several considerations render such a view less compelling
than it appears at first sight. First of all it must be questioned
whether the material contained in Exodus 15:22–18:27 can be
regarded as a cycle of Kadesh stories. Of the several stories
contained in this complex only Exodus 17:1–7, with its reference
to Massah and Meribah (*v.* 7), shows a connection with Kadesh.
But it is not at all clear that the Marah story, narrated in Exodus
15:22–5a, has any association with Kadesh, and the same is true
also of the story of the quails and manna in Exodus 16. As for the
meeting between Israel and the Midianites recorded in Exodus 18,
it takes place at 'the mountain of God' and, as Noth has argued,
there is no need to doubt that this reference belongs to the original
details of the tradition here narrated.[71] In reality it seems that
what we have in Exodus 15:22–18:27 is a rather loosely connected series of originally self-contained stories and that accordingly, as Noth again has pointed out, the local associations of these
stories may not be transferred from one to another.[72] They cannot

[69] That is the most natural interpretation of the phrase 'and brought
you to myself' (*v.* 4).
[70] Ps. 78 goes up to the election of David.
[71] M. Noth, *Exodus*, 147f.   [72] Ibid., 147.

therefore be termed a cycle of Kadesh stories, for only one of them may be associated with this location.[73] If this is the case we can no longer think of the Sinai story as being superimposed upon an earlier so-called Exodus-Kadesh narrative; rather, a Sinai story (though not of course the elaborate JE Sinai narrative in Exodus 19ff.) may well have belonged to this complex in Exodus 15:22–18:27 from the beginning or at least from an early stage. To put the same point another way: some sort of Sinai story is no less likely to have had a place in such a complex than any of the other narratives we now find in it.[74]

For all these reasons, therefore, von Rad's view that the so-called settlement tradition was originally quite independent of the Sinai tradition must be rejected. And we may note that this has serious consequences for Noth's views, since his own reconstruction of the early history of the Exodus and Sinai traditions is very largely dependent upon von Rad's conclusions. We may observe also, with regard to Noth's work, that recent research has shown that his theory of an early Israelite amphictyony is highly questionable, which means in turn that his presentation of the history of the Pentateuchal traditions and their gradual combination into G, a presentation inseparably bound up with his theory of an amphictyony and its central shrines, must be rejected.[75] At the same time his suggestion that the J and E narratives presuppose an earlier Pentateuchal narrative G remains entirely plausible, though the process whereby it came into existence will require reinvestigation.

IV

Of the other scholars during the past generation who also hold that the Exodus and Sinai traditions were originally, and for a

[73] Indeed it is not impossible that this story itself was not originally associated with Kadesh. Both it and the story of the battle with the Amalekites which follows it (Exod. 17:8ff.) are associated with Rephidim and it is worth asking whether the very nature of the story in Exod. 17:1–7, centring as it does on a *rib* between Moses and Israel, may have attracted the reference to Massah and Meribah (why two names?) from elsewhere (cf. Deut. 33:8; Ps. 95:8).

[74] Cf. J. M. Schmidt, 'Erwägungen zum Verhältnis von Auszugs- und Sinaitradition', *ZAW* 82 (1970), 23.

[75] For a recent discussion of Noth's theory of an amphictyony see G. W. Anderson, 'Israel: Amphictyony: 'AM; KĀHĀL; 'ĒDÂH', in *Translating and Understanding the Old Testament*, ed. H. Thomas Frank and W. L. Reed, New York–Nashville 1970, 135–51.

greater or lesser length of time, independent of one another almost all,[76] as far as I am aware, do so very largely on the basis of von Rad's conclusions to which they add for the most part only minor additional observations.[77] With all these we need not concern ourselves here.

Brief mention must be made, however, of one further full-scale

[76] This is true also of the work of H.- J. Kraus, 'Gilgal: ein Beitrag zur Kultusgeschichte Israels', *VT* 1 (1951), 181–99; cf. his *Worship in Israel*, E.T. by G. Buswell, Oxford 1966, 152ff., who accepts von Rad's view of the original independence of the Sinai tradition from the settlement tradition and is concerned primarily with the problem of how the two traditions were eventually united. He believes, contrary to von Rad, that their combination was already brought about in Israel's cult in the pre-monarchial period. He finds evidence in Josh. 2–6 of a cultic festival at Gilgal celebrating the conquest and involving a procession in which the ark was carried across the Jordan as a re-enactment of the crossing of the Reed Sea. The festival took place in the spring (at the feast of Passover-Unleavened Bread). The place of the ark in the festival points to a time, he maintains, when the central sanctuary of the amphictyony had moved from Shechem to Gilgal. This in turn means, he contends, that the covenant traditions of Shechem moved to Gilgal and were there united with the *Landnahme* traditions in the cult. But apart from the difficulty of accepting such a procession through the waters of the Jordan (how was it done?) various serious objections have been raised against this hypothesis: (1) even if there was an amphictyony, it is extremely doubtful whether Gilgal was ever one of its central sanctuaries; (2) it has been cogently disputed whether the ark was an original constituent of the narrative of Josh. 3–5; (3) the crossing of the Reed Sea is referred to only in Josh. 4:23 and even then in a rather incidental manner, a fact hardly in keeping with the emphasis placed upon this motif by Kraus in the alleged festival (cf. M. Noth, *Joshua*, 33). Various arguments against Kraus's theory are summarized in a paper on the background of Josh. 3–5 read by Prof. J. R. Porter to the Society for Old Testament Study in Oxford 1971 and now published in *SEÅ* 36 (1971), 5–23.

[77] A notable exception to this is the work of C. A. Simpson, *The Early Traditions of Israel*, Oxford 1948, where the original independence of the Exodus and Sinai traditions from each other is argued on the basis of a detailed literary-critical analysis of the earliest Pentateuchal narratives. Simpson isolates a J[1] from a J[2] narrative and concludes (cf. ibid., 419ff.) that the J[2] traditions had nothing to do with the Exodus which was experienced by the J[1] group who were centred at Kadesh and whose leader was Moses. Both traditions were combined by the author of J[2] who used the J[1] narrative as the basis of his own more elaborate work. But Simpson's literary analysis, in places highly subjective, and his conclusions have met with little support. For a detailed critique of his work see O. Eissfeldt, *Die älttesten Traditionen Israels. Ein kritischer Bericht über C. A. Simpson's The Early Traditions of Israel*, BZAW 71 (1950).

work which advances conclusions similar to those of von Rad but
on the basis of different evidence. The work in question comes
from the Swiss scholar, H. Wildberger.[78] His work is remarkably
similar in method to von Rad's: he finds what he believes to be an
ancient text embodying a recitation of the saving history but in
which the Sinai tradition is not represented; he believes the text in
question to have had its basis in and to reflect the form of a recurring cultic festival in early Israel; he identifies the festival in
question and finally discusses how and when the Sinai tradition
was connected with the traditions of this festival.

He fully accepts von Rad's view that the Sinai tradition had its
original *Sitz im Leben* in an ancient Israelite covenant renewal
festival celebrated periodically at Shechem at the feast of Tabernacles. Wildberger is mainly concerned, however, with the nature
and *Sitz im Leben* of the so-called settlement tradition and on both
of these questions arrives at conclusions quite different from those
of von Rad.

His own point of departure is Exodus 19:3b-8 which he classifies
as a proclamation of Israel's election. Its present context is of
course the Sinai pericope but it is maintained that its association
with this context is secondary and late. From a literary point of
view, Wildberger rejects any suggestion that it comes from the
Priestly authors or a Deuteronomic redactor, even though he
concedes that it has some contacts in phraseology with Deuteronomy. The possibility that the passage belongs to J or E is
doubted on the grounds that it disturbs the JE narrative in Exodus
19. The passage is, Wildberger argues, an ancient formulation of
Israel's election tradition. He analyses the structure of the passage
as follows:[79] (1) introduction (*v.* 3b); (2) recollection of the saving
history (*v.* 4); (3) call for obedience to Yahweh's commands
(*v.* 5a); (4) the proclamation of Israel's election (*vv.* 5b-6a); (5)
the commitment of the people (*vv.* 7-8).

Wildberger then makes several observations about this text and
its component parts as set out above. Firstly, he argues that *v.* 5a
(his section 3), 'Now therefore, if you obey my voice and keep my
covenant', is a secondary insertion into the passage. He finds
parallels between it and similar formulae in the Deuteronomic and
related literature and argues further that the mention of the

---

[78] H. Wildberger, *Jahwes Eigentumsvolk*, ATANT 37 (Zürich
1960).

[79] Ibid., 14f.

covenant is in any case an anachronism since the Sinai covenant has
has not yet been made and the appeal for obedience to it is therefore premature. Secondly, he believes that the recitation of the
Heilsgeschichte in *v.* 4 (his section 2) is only part of a larger tradition
complex, that is, Israel's election tradition (*Erwählungstradition*).
For this reason he argues, against von Rad, that it is wrong to begin
with the so-called creed in Deuteronomy 26:5b–9 and its related
texts elsewhere. He maintains that whilst it is true that the Deuteronomic authors have taken up and used old traditions in composing
their book, in doing so they have employed them quite freely and
have not hesitated to unite elements of tradition which were
originally separate or to separate elements of tradition which
originally belonged together.[80] Finally, Wildberger believes that
we have in Exodus 19:3b–8 a description of a cultic celebration:
God's spokesman, the mediator (here Moses), receives his instructions from God and conveys the divine proclamation to the
elders, the representatives of Israel; the elders bind themselves in
the name of the people to observe what God says and the mediator
conveys their response to God. He then proceeds to investigate the
Sitz im Leben of such a festival, rejecting von Rad's claim that the
Heilsgeschichte themes were associated with the feast of Weeks and
arguing that the election festival was celebrated on the occasion of
the feast of Unleavened Bread at Gilgal. Subsequently he argues
that the Sinai tradition was associated with the election tradition
by an author and though accepting that the Yahwist could have
been the author in question he prefers Noth's view that they were
combined at a time before the Yahwist worked and most probably
by the authors of G, as Noth suggests.

Wildberger's thesis stands or falls on the question whether his
assessment of the nature and origin of Exodus 19:3b–8 is correct.
In fact, however, it seems highly doubtful whether this text was
originally an independent unit. It may well be an insertion into this
chapter (most commentators agree that it is) but if it is, it was
composed precisely for its present context. Thus the recollection
of the saving history which it contains mentions only the Exodus
and by implication the journey to Sinai (this surely is the meaning
of 'I brought you to *myself*') and goes no further and it would be
quite arbitrary to suppose that it once contained a longer and more
comprehensive recital of the *Heilsgeschichte* which mentioned also
the settlement in Canaan. Furthermore, the presence in it of

[80] Ibid., 33.

Deuteronomic phraseology[81] suggests that it was composed and placed in its present context by a Deuteronomic redactor from whom not a few other glosses and insertions observable elsewhere in the Tetrateuch derive. Wildberger would of course excise *v*. 5a, which has a marked Deuteronomic flavour. But precisely here he raises a major difficulty for his own thesis. It will be recalled that he regards *vv*. 7–8 (his section 5) as constituting the commitment of the people following the proclamation of Israel's election in *vv*. 5b–6a (section 4). But commitment to what? Surely when the people respond 'all that Yahweh has spoken *we will do*' it can only be understood as a commitment to obey the covenant law and thus clearly presupposes *v*. 5a. In this respect we may point to the same procedure in Exodus 24:3ff. where the people's commitment—we observe that much the same terminology is employed: 'all the words which Yahweh has spoken we will do'—clearly presupposes the announcement by Moses of the divine law. We may note one further criticism which may be levelled against Wildberger's work. He criticizes von Rad's use of material from Deuteronomy to establish his particular viewpoint on the grounds that the Deuteronomic authors have used old traditions in too free a manner. Yet, unless I have mistaken Wildberger's own arguments, he himself points to a number of texts from the prophetic literature in which he finds evidence of the persistence of the alleged erstwhile independence of the Sinai tradition from the so-called election tradition.[82] How less free, we are bound to ask, were the prophets in their use of the old traditions than the Deuteronomic authors?

The matter cannot of course be left here. Various fundamental issues arise for discussion and re-investigation. We shall obviously have to examine the JE narrative of the Sinai events in Exodus 19ff., for it has become clear from our discussion in the foregoing pages that it antedates the passages cited by von Rad in his investigation. What information can be gained from this material concerning the original basis and content of the Sinai tradition and its possible connection with or independence from the Exodus tradition? What conclusions can be drawn from an investigation of it with regard to the origin of the covenant between Yahweh and Israel? We shall return to these and other questions later.

The rejection of the case advanced by von Rad and others for

[81] Cf. M. Noth, *Exodus*, 157f. See further below 64, n. 27.
[82] H. Wildberger, op. cit., 63f.

the separation of the Exodus and Sinai traditions in early Israel
leads us at this stage to a consideration of the work of a number of
scholars who have argued precisely the opposite point of view, viz.
that both traditions belonged together from the earliest period and
had a common *Sitz im Leben* in early Israel. We now turn to a
discussion of this point of view. Once again, however, it is not my
intention to discuss every one of the many contributions advocating
this particular view. I have endeavoured simply to present the main
arguments in favour of it and have concentrated on what I believe
to be the major and most representative works in which it is
advanced.

2

Exodus, Covenant and Treaty

I

We begin with the work of A. Weiser who has consistently and vigorously challenged the view that the Sinai and Exodus traditions were originally independent of each other, arguing instead that they belonged together from the earliest period as component parts of one and the same cultic festival in ancient Israel.[1] Weiser accepts the view that a covenant renewal festival was periodically celebrated in pre-monarchical Israel and associates it, at least in its earliest stages, with Shechem. He agrees also with von Rad in seeking the roots of the Pentateuchal tradition in the festival cult of early Israel. But beyond this he has subjected von Rad's thesis to serious criticism and we have already had occasion to note some of the observations he makes against von Rad's views. Thus he rejects the use von Rad makes of the so-called creed in Deuteronomy 26:5b–9. He questions whether the presentation of 'the first of all the fruit of the ground' at the sanctuary, with the accompanying confession relating this liturgical occasion to Yahweh's saving acts, did take place at the feast of Weeks, observing that in Deuteronomy 26:1ff. there is no mention at all of a feast as the appointed time and arguing that the whole context runs counter to von Rad's view that the feast of Weeks may be tacitly implied. 'It is just as possible', he contends, 'and, judging by the context and the subject matter (the first of *all* the fruit of the ground), more likely that different offerings at different times unrelated to any particular feast, are meant here.'[2]

As to the absence of any reference to the Sinai event in the recitation of the *Heilsgeschichte*, Weiser agrees with von Rad that a

[1] A. Weiser, *Introduction to the Old Testament*, 81–99.
[2] Ibid., 84.

distinction exists between the Sinai tradition with its theophany
and its covenant making on the one hand and the tradition of
Yahweh's saving deeds as historical events on the other, but he
rejects von Rad's conclusion from this that there would not have
been room for both these traditions side by side in one and the
same festival and that they must have belonged to two separate
cultic occasions.[3] As we saw earlier, Weiser argues persuasively
that the Sinai tradition is not a historical event in the same sense
as the historical events of the Exodus and the conquest: 'It (the
Sinai event) is on the contrary an encounter with God which leads
up to the acceptance by the people of the will of God proclaimed
in the commandments; and in its cultic setting it represents a
particular action in the course of the festival.'[4] For Weiser the
revelation of God's nature in his saving acts in history, the
Heilsgeschichte, and the revelation of his will leading up to the
pledge of the congregation (the covenant ceremony proper) were
two parts of one and the same cultic occasion, the festival of the
renewal of the covenant. Accordingly, he regards von Rad's
deductions from such disparate elements of tradition as are found
in Exodus 19, Deuteronomy 26:5b–9; 27, as well as Psalms and
hymns which celebrate Yahweh's deeds of salvation in history (e.g.
Exod. 15; Pss. 44:2ff.; 77:12ff; 78:2ff.; 105; 136; etc.) as inadmissible: 'It cannot be expected of such separate parts of the festal
liturgy that they should present the entire substance of the festal
performance, especially as the subject of the hymn is usually
concerned with Yahweh's acts of salvation as proofs of the divine
greatness and power. The Sinai tradition, on the other hand, with
its pledge of the cult-congregation to the proclamation of the
divine will is outside the range of vision of these hymns; yet this
does not allow the conclusion to be drawn that this tradition could
not have had a place at another point in the festal liturgy.'[5]

To substantiate this view, Weiser points to Samuel's speech in
1 Samuel 12 which he relates to the festival tradition, arguing that
it presupposes the covenant obligations (cf. *vv.* 9, 10) and that the
demand for Israel's obedience to the covenant actually forms its
main purpose (cf. *vv.* 14f.). 'But if the fundamental idea of the
Sinai tradition runs like a red thread through the whole speech', he
concludes, 'then naturally a special mention of the "Sinai events"
would be superfluous.'[6]

---

[3] Ibid., 85f.	[4] Ibid., 86.	[5] Ibid., 87.	[6] Ibid., 87.

More important still, however, Weiser believes that Joshua 24 goes back to an early tradition[7] in which there is a clear juxtaposition of the recollection of Yahweh's saving deeds (*vv.* 2–13) *and* the people's commitment to the covenant (*vv.* 14–26).[8] If behind Joshua 24 there lies, as Noth and von Rad have argued, a recurring ceremony of covenant-making in early Israel, then, Weiser contends, the combination of the recollection of God's saving activity in history and the pledge of the people to the covenant can be understood 'only if "history and law" were from the earliest days the two fundamental pillars of the tradition in one and the same cult festival for the sacral union of the tribes of All-Israel'.[9]

Weiser therefore argues that the combination of the two sets of tradition was not effected by the Yahwist, as von Rad believes, but was handed down to the Yahwist as 'an established datum'.[10] And he points further to passages which cannot be regarded as dependent upon the Yahwist and in which this combination of the two traditions is presupposed (cf. Exod. 3:18; 19:3ff.; Deut. 6:20ff.; 1 Sam. 7:14f.; Pss. 44:2ff.; 81:6ff.; 97:10ff.; 111:4, 6f.; Jer. 7:22ff.; 31:31ff.).[11]

Throughout his work Weiser expressed caution on the possibility of reconstructing the procedure of the covenant festival in any detail and contented himself with apprehending some of its basic elements. On the basis of fresh evidence, however, a number of scholars have gone further and have attempted not only to substantiate Weiser's basic thesis concerning the relationship between the *Heilsgeschichte* and the Sinai covenant tradition in the Old Testament but also to reconstruct in more detail the actual structure of the covenant and the component parts of the covenant festival in which they believe it had its original home in early Israel. The new evidence in question has come from investigations into the form and content of international vassal or suzerainty

---

[7] The recitation of the *Heilsgeschichte* is here presented in the first person singular form of address as the direct speech of Yahweh and is thus, he argues, more original than, e.g., Deut. 26:5b–9. Is it really clear, however, that the mere fact of a speech being formulated as a direct speech of God is necessarily an indication that such a speech is earlier than other speeches not so formulated?

[8] A. Weiser, op. cit., 87.   [9] Ibid., 88.   [10] Ibid., 89.

[11] Ibid., 89. It is by no means certain, however, that some of these texts do not presuppose the JE narrative in the Pentateuch. The authors of almost all of them could have been in possession of the JE narrative.

treaties from the Hittite empire of the late Bronze Age (1450–1200 B.C.). At a later stage in our study we shall see that yet more treaty material from the Assyrian empire of the middle of the first millennium B.C. has shed further light on the covenant form in the Old Testament and has led to some major modifications of earlier conclusions arrived at solely on the basis of the Hittite treaties. At this stage, however, we shall concern ourselves only with the work done on the basis of the Hittite material. In doing so I shall concentrate primarily on the work of W. Beyerlin,[12] for although many other important studies of the Sinai covenant tradition in the light of the Hittite treaties have been made in recent years,[13] for our present purposes none has been more thoroughgoing than his, and as far as the relationship between the Exodus and covenant traditions are concerned the works of other scholars on the basis of these treaties are in substantial agreement with Beyerlin's conclusions. Since, however, the initial work on the light shed by the Hittite treaties on the Sinai covenant tradition was done by the American scholar G. E. Mendenhall,[14] we must begin with a review of his pioneering contribution.

II

Mendenhall's notable essay on the origin, nature and form of the Sinai covenant in the light of Hittite suzerainty treaties was published in 1954 and constituted a major turning point in the investigation of the problem with which we are concerned. He begins with an observation concerning what he believes to be the place and function of a covenant in the origins and early history of Israel: 'The real historical problem involved', he states, 'is not one which concerns the pre-Mosaic religious ideas so much as the question of the pre-Mosaic relationships which existed between the various groups who became Israel. If, as Israelite tradition maintained, there were only descendants of Abraham, Isaac, and Jacob, in short a group bound together by blood-ties or a clan,

---

[12] W. Beyerlin, *Origins and History of the Oldest Sinaitic Traditions*, E.T. by S. Rudman, Oxford 1965.

[13] For a survey of the discussion see esp. D. J. McCarthy, *Old Testament Covenant*, Oxford 1972, where also an extensive bibliography is provided.

[14] G. E. Mendenhall, 'Covenant Forms in Israelite Tradition', *BA* 17 (1954), 50–76.

then it is not so likely that a covenant would have been necessary to bind them together as a religious group. Rather, as Wellhausen maintained, the original relationship of the group to Yahweh as well as to each other, would have been a "natural" one, and therefore the covenant idea must have been a much later development of religious thought.'[15] But few today would accept, he then points out, that Israel emerged in the genealogical fashion described in the Old Testament whereby the people's solidarity derived from blood-ties.[16] This being so, it follows, he further maintains, 'that the covenant relationship between Israel and Yahweh which is inseparable from the solidarity of the tribes, is not merely a stage in the history of religious concepts, but was an *event* which had a definite historical setting and the most surprising consequences.'[17] That is to say, he argues that the covenant functioned sociologically and institutionally as the means whereby originally disparate groups of people, whether clans or tribes, were brought together into a common relationship with each other. The problem arises therefore, as Mendenhall sees it, of arriving at a 'concept of a covenant which would bind together the tribes and also adequately form a foundation for the normative conception that in this event Yahweh became the God of Israel'.[18]

It is with this problem that Mendenhall is primarily concerned in his essay in which he argues that there was a type of covenant in the ancient Near East, viz. the suzerainty treaty by which a great king bound his vassals to faithfulness and obedience to himself, on the basis of which a solution to this problem may be found. The treaties, as we have already noted, derive from the state archives of the Hittite empire of the late Bronze Age[19] and as such were contemporary with the beginnings of the people of Israel, a fact which is seized upon as highly significant by Mendenhall and many others. Mendenhall defends his use of such international treaties from Hatti as a means of shedding light on the Biblical covenant material on the following grounds.

[15] Ibid., 50f.
[16] Nevertheless a re-investigation of ethnic ties as the real binding factor among the early Israelites should now be undertaken, especially in view of the fact that Noth's theory of an amphictyony no longer appears to provide a satisfactory explanation of the relations between the tribes.
[17] G. E. Mendenhall, op. cit., 51.   [18] Ibid., 51.
[19] The Hittite treaties were investigated by V. Korošec, *Hethitische Staatsverträge*, Leipzig 1931.

(*a*) The Hittites themselves did not create the treaty-form but borrowed or inherited it as an already well established form in the ancient Near East and deriving ultimately from Mesopotamia. It was an international form and would have been familiar to the peoples and states in the second millennium B.C.

(*b*) A number of these treaties were made with Syrian states and the form was also employed in making a treaty with Egypt. Furthermore, he continues, the Israelite traditions, now vindicated, indicate close relationships between the pre-Mosaic peoples, who became Israel, and northern Mesopotamia so that 'abundant opportunity to become familiar with the treaty form must be admitted for ancient Israel'.[20]

(*c*) A number of other and independent parallels between Hittite and Israelite laws and customs have already been observed.

(*d*) The argument that the pre-Mosaic tribes were much too primitive a group to have been familiar with such a highly developed form is rejected by Mendenhall. He questions the widely accepted view that the Israelite clans or tribes were originally semi-nomadic groups, arguing that neither Abraham or Jacob was a typical nomad. Properly understood, he maintains, they are Hebrews (*habiru*), as indeed the Bible describes them, that is, 'outsiders who have no legal status, and as heads of roving bands who have covenant relationships with the city-states of Palestine'.[21]

Turning to an examination of the structure of these Hittite treaties, Mendenhall finds that although the form is not rigid and the order and wording of its different parts not always the same, the following six elements nearly always are found in them:[22]

1. *Preamble.* The king identifies himself, listing his titles and other attributes as well as his genealogy. This preamble, Mendenhall suggests, emphasizes the majesty and power of the suzerain who is conferring a covenant relationship upon his vassals.

2. *Historical prologue.* Here the previous relations between the suzerain and the vassal are described, great emphasis being placed upon the benevolent deeds which the Hittite king has wrought in times past on behalf of the vassal. This historical prologue, it is

---

[20] G. E. Mendenhall, op. cit., 54.

[21] This view is further developed by Mendenhall in 'The Hebrew Conquest of Palestine', *BA* 25 (1962), 66–96. For a discussion of his views expressed here see M. Weippert, *The Settlement of the Israelite Tribes in Palestine*, E.T. by J. D. Martin, London 1971, 55ff., 63ff.

[22] G. E. Mendenhall, 'Covenant Forms in Israelite Tradition', 58ff.

argued, was intended to evoke the vassal's gratitude towards the suzerain, a gratitude which would manifest itself in loyalty and faithfulness to the overlord. It is followed by:

3. *The treaty stipulations.* The obligations binding upon the vassal are here presented. Mendenhall lists a number of typical laws, amongst them, for example, the stipulation that the vassal is not to enter into foreign relationships outside the Hittite empire, the prohibition of any misdeeds against other people under the sovereignty of the Hittite king, and the command that the vassal must appear once a year before his Hittite overlord.

4. *Provision for depositing of the treaty document in the vassal's temple and for the periodic reading of it.* The requirement that the text of the treaty was to be read periodically by the vassal was intended to insure that the subject state remained constantly aware of its obligations to the treaty overlord. The deposit of the treaty document in the vassal's temple perhaps indicated that it was under the divine protection of the vassal's own gods as a further warning against breach of treaty.

5. *The list of gods as witnesses.* In this section the gods who witnessed the making of the treaty are listed. They include the gods of both the suzerain and the vassal and it is they who protect the treaty. Mendenhall draws particular attention, however, to the inclusion among these witnesses of the (deified) mountains, rivers, springs, sea, heaven and earth, the winds and the clouds.

6. *The curses and blessings formulae.* The purpose of this section speaks for itself. The gods who protect the treaty will bring disaster upon the vassal in the event of a breach of the treaty. On the other hand the vassal's loyalty to the overlord will bring continued blessings upon him and his people.

In concluding this part of his study, Mendenhall stresses that this particular treaty-form is not found in any period subsequent to the second millennium. It may be expected that the treaty structure in question outlasted the Hittite empire, but 'it is perfectly clear that the home of this form is in the second millennium B.C. and cannot be proven (outside Israel) to have survived elsewhere'.[23]

On the basis of this Mendenhall proceeds to an examination of the Biblical material concerning the covenant at Sinai in which Moses played a vital role.[24] He centres his discussion on the Decalogue, and prefaces it with a number of observations. Firstly,

[23] Ibid., 61.   [24] Ibid., 61ff.

he fully emphasizes the role of Moses as the one who bound together the disparate clans and tribes who were to form Israel. Secondly, he affirms the view that the unity of the tribes thus achieved by Moses was religious and not political. Thirdly, he reminds us that the Israelite tribes were not an ethnically homogeneous group with a common ancestry. Already in the desert they were 'a mixed multitude' (cf. Num. 11:4) whilst later, after this group had entered the land of Canaan, 'whole groups of the population of Palestine must have entered *en bloc* into the Israelite federation'.[25] Finally, he adopts Noth's view that the earliest organization of the tribes was that of a religious federation based on a common allegiance to Yahweh and with a central sanctuary as a further unifying factor in their life together. And he concludes: 'All these elements in the traditions of Israel hold together and indeed make sense only on the supposition that there actually was a covenant relation at the basis of the system.'[26] The covenant was therefore the means whereby the diverse clans who left Egypt under the leadership of Moses were made into a community and, according to Mendenhall, we have the text of that covenant in the Decalogue, apart of course from the material in it which can be shown to be a later addition.

In forming the community Moses, it is then argued, adopted the suzerainty treaty, the elements of which Mendenhall finds in the Decalogue, though only partly, and elsewhere in the Mosaic traditions in the Old Testament. Thus the first clause of the Decalogue is regarded as the historical prologue describing the previous relationship between Yahweh, the divine Overlord and King, and his people Israel: 'I am Yahweh your God who brought you forth from the land of Egypt' (Exod. 20:2). Again, as in the Hittite treaties, this prologue is taken as establishing the obligations which Israel has towards her divine benefactor Yahweh. This is followed by the covenant stipulations, the Ten Commandments (Exod. 20:3ff.), to which the people would have pledged themselves (cf. Exod. 19:8). There would also have been, it is further argued, a ceremony ratifying the covenant, such as the sprinkling of blood on the altar and on the people (Exod. 24:5ff.) or the banquet eaten by Moses and the seventy elders in the presence of Yahweh on the mountain (Exod. 24:9ff.).

[25] For this see especially Mendenhall's study, 'The Hebrew Conquest of Palestine', 66–96.
[26] G. E. Mendenhall, 'Covenant Forms in Israelite Tradition', 63.

Mendenhall acknowledges that the Decalogue itself does not present a complete parallel to the suzerainty treaty-form; it lacks, for example, the provision for the depositing of the covenant document in the sanctuary; nor does it contain a list of witnesses or include blessings and curses formulae. But these elements are found by Mendenhall elsewhere in the Mosaic traditions.[27] Furthermore, he finds the form more fully represented in Joshua 24 which he regards, following Noth and others, as being based upon an ancient tradition going back to a period when the treaty-form was still a living institution, even though in its present form it represents a later adaptation of this old tradition.[28]

We need not pursue the parallels thus found by Mendenhall between the Sinai covenant tradition and the suzerainty treaties any further, since the main point as far as our present purposes are concerned has already been arrived at, viz. Mendenhall's observation that the so-called election tradition, the nucleus and basis of which was the deliverance from bondage in Egypt, had a vital place within the covenant structure, forming the historical prologue to the presentation of the covenant law: '"history" and "law" were bound up into an organic unit from the very beginnings of Israel itself. Since the cultus was at least connected with the covenant proclamation or renewal, we can see that in early Israel, history, cultus, and "law" were inseparable. . . .'[29]

Such a conclusion, if it can be sustained, is obviously of the utmost significance for the problem with which we are concerned in this study. From the point of view of the history of traditions it indicates that there was from the earliest period in Israel's history a close connection between the *Heilsgeschichte*, the original element and crystallization point of which was the Exodus, and

---

[27] Thus he believes that the depositing of the 'tables' of the law in the ark (cf. Deut. 10:1–5; 1 Kgs. 8:9) reflects the procedure in the case of the treaties (op. cit., 64). As to the list of witnesses typical of the suzerainty treaties, the absence of these, including as they do various deities, is not to be wondered at in the Old Testament. Nevertheless, Mendenhall refers to such texts as Deut. 32:1 and Isa. 1:2 (cf. also Mic. 6:1–2) in which 'heaven and earth', 'mountains' and 'hills' are summoned as witnesses. As to the blessings and curses formulae, they do form part of early Israelite legal tradition and their place in the covenant tradition is indicated by Deut. 28 (op. cit., 60, 66).

[28] On Josh. 24 see his 'Covenant Forms in Israelite Tradition', 67ff. and also his 'The Hebrew Conquest of Palestine', 84ff.

[29] G. E. Mendenhall, 'Covenant Forms in Israelite Tradition', 70.

the Sinai covenant, whilst from a historical point of view it points
to a direct relationship between the events of Exodus and Sinai in
the formation of the people of Israel.

Such was the weight and importance of Mendenhall's original
thesis that a great number of studies by other scholars followed it,
further developing its relevance for our understanding of the
nature and form of the Sinai covenant as well as its significance for
the relationship between the historical traditions and the covenant
tradition in Israel. Amongst these one of the most notable is the
work of W. Beyerlin which comprises a detailed and thoroughgoing elaboration of Mendenhall's work, further drawing out and
exemplifying its significance for an understanding of the origins
and early history of the Exodus and Sinai traditions and their
Sitz im Leben in early Israel.[30] In what follows we shall summarize
briefly the main points made by Beyerlin, after which we shall turn
to various criticisms which have been levelled against the use made
by him and Mendenhall of the Hittite treaties, and the relevance
for the problem of more recent research into ancient Near Eastern
treaties, especially those from the Assyrian empire of the first
millennium B.C.

Before proceeding, however, one question may here be raised
with regard to Mendenhall's remarks noted above concerning the
function of the covenant in the formation of early Israel, that is, his
view that such a covenant would have been the means whereby
originally separate and independent groups of people were bound
together. That a covenant would have been one means of uniting
separate groups of people need not be questioned. But the question
which Mendelhall does not appear to raise is why Israel's covenant
was between Israel and Yahweh. In other words, Mendenhall's
point of view requires only that a covenant was made between
separate groups of people in which, it might be assumed, Yahweh
as their common God would have acted as divine guarantor in
whose presence such a covenant would have been made. But such a
covenant would not have required that Yahweh himself was to be
one of the 'contracting' parties involved in making it. Why Israel's
covenant was not simply a covenant between various groups of
people, as Mendenhall's understanding of its function seems to
mean, but a covenant between these groups and Yahweh, a
covenant in which Yahweh was involved as a 'contracting' party,
so to speak, remains unexplained by Mendenhall's theory. We

[30] W. Beyerlin, *Origins and History of the Oldest Sinaitic Traditions.*

shall have occasion to comment on this issue at a later stage in our
investigation.

III

Beyerlin's work presents a detailed investigation of the nature and
form of the Sinai covenant tradition and seeks to trace its origins,
history and development from the pre-settlement period through
the pre-monarchical period to the monarchical period itself. His
study comprises three sections, the first dealing with the literary
analysis of the Sinai tradition as presented in the JE narrative in
Exodus 19–24, 32–34, the second with a traditio-historical
investigation of this material, and the third presenting a summary
and conclusion comprising a reconstruction of the origins and
history of the tradition. It is with the second and third sections that
we shall be concerned.

In his second section Beyerlin seeks to determine the factors
which shaped the separate elements of the Sinai tradition in their
pre-literary stage as well as to discover their particular *Sitz im
Leben*. From this traditio-historical enquiry he concludes that the
dominant influence in shaping the tradition as a whole was
Israel's cult. That is to say, following Weiser, he points to a
recurring festival of covenant renewal in early Israel as the *Sitz im
Leben* in which the tradition took shape and developed. Thus, for
example, the account of the purificatory rites (Exod. 19:10–11a,
14–15a, 15b) reflect, he believes, a sacral tradition concerning the
preparation for worship and the epiphany of Yahweh in the festal
cult. Similarly, he argues that the cloud of smoke which conceals
Yahweh from the congregation has its basis in an incense rite
(Exod. 19:9, 16, 18; 20:18; 33:9; 34:5. Cf. Lev. 16:2, 12, 13;
Isa. 6:4; 1 Kgs. 8:10). Likewise, he argues that the sounding of
the trumpet frequently alluded to (Exod. 19:13b, 16, 19; 20:18)
corresponds to the practice of blowing the trumpet at the cultic
theophany, possibly as a means of portraying the voice of God. The
proclamation of the name of Yahweh is believed to reflect the
practice of invoking the divine name to help 'actualize' the theophany (Exod. 33:19; 34:5f.). Beyerlin draws attention to the
act of obeisance (Exod. 33:10; 34:8) as further evidence of the
cultic background of this material. Similarly, the eating of a
covenant meal (Exod. 24:9–11) as well as the rite of sprinkling the

blood of sacrificial victims on the people and the altar (Exod. 24:3ff.) point to a cultic occasion and *Sitz im Leben*. The proclamation of the divine commands, the covenant law (Exod. 20:2–17, the Decalogue), is likewise placed within the context of a cultic act; Beyerlin further contends that the parenetic expansion of the original apodictic commands took place within a liturgical setting.[31] Finally, he draws attention to the fixing of a time and place for Yahweh's epiphany (Exod. 19:10f.; 34:24; 19:12–13a, 20–4; 34:3) as well as the appointment and role of a covenant mediator (Exod. 20:18–21; cf. 19:9) as additional evidence of the cultic celebration of the covenant and the influence of the cult upon the development and transmission of the tradition.

Of particular relevance for us, however, is Beyerlin's discussion of the Decalogue in Exodus 20:2–17.[32] This he begins by affirming, firstly, the view of Mowinckel and von Rad that the Decalogue had its *Sitz im Leben* in a cultic festival, and secondly the view of Alt that the apodictic laws which form the basis of the Decalogue originated in the cult.[33] But the question with which Beyerlin is primarily concerned is 'where the form which lies at the basis of the Decalogue *as a whole* originated',[34] and it is here that he takes up Mendenhall's brief assessment of the nature and structure of the Decalogue in the light of the Hittite suzerainty treaties.[35] The correspondences which he finds between the Decalogue and the treaty-form are substantially the same as those set out by Mendenhall, though presented in more detail, and we need not repeat them here. At the same time Beyerlin's analysis goes beyond Mendenhall's in some significant respects. Thus, for example, he believes the preamble to the Hittite treaty-form in which the suzerain as author and lord of the treaty announces himself is paralleled by the first clause of the Decalogue 'I am Yahweh, your God. . . .' (Exod. 20:2a). Similarly, he believes the designation of the treaty stipulations as the suzerain's 'words' to be paralleled by the

[31] W. Beyerlin, op. cit., 49ff. Cf. also his 'Die Paränese im Bundesbuch und ihre Herkunft', *Gottes Wort und Gottes Land*, Festschrift for H. W. Hertzberg, ed. by H. Graf Reventlow, Göttingen 1965, 9–29.

[32] W. Beyerlin, *Origins and History of the Oldest Sinaitic Traditions*, 49–67.

[33] Ibid., 50. Cf. A. Alt, 'The Origins of Israelite Law', in *Essays on Old Testament History and Religion*, E.T. by R. A. Wilson, Oxford 1966, 81–132.

[34] W. Beyerlin, *Origins and History of the Oldest Sinaitic Traditions*, 50.

[35] Ibid., 50ff.

description of the Decalogue as Yahweh's 'words': 'And God spake all these *words*' (Exod. 20:1). Most important of all, however, is the fact that whereas Mendenhall found nothing in the Decalogue corresponding to the blessings and curses formulae in the Hittite treaties, Beyerlin argues that the commandments themselves as apodictic formulations setting forth categorical prohibitions are by their very nature absolute and *ipso facto* the most powerful sanctions: 'The categorical and unconditional nature of the Ten Commandments really contains within itself the same judgement of death or curse on disobedience that is expressed in other apodictic sequences by a *môt yûmāt* or *'ārûr*.'[36] Beyerlin thus concludes that the most important elements in the structure of the Decalogue follow the Hittite treaty-form and considers it 'proven that the formal structure of the Decalogue should not be considered as Israel's creation but as modelled on this existing, well-established treaty-form'.[37]

The conclusions drawn by Beyerlin from his traditio-historical investigation of the Sinai tradition in Exodus 19–24, 32–4 are presented in the third and final section of his work where he attempts to trace the development of the tradition (a) in the desert period; (b) in the period between the invasion of Palestine and the formation of the state; and (c) in the period of the monarchy. For our purposes it is the first of these which is most relevant.

Here the conclusion already arrived at by Mendenhall with regard to the relationship of the Exodus tradition to the Sinai covenant tradition is reaffirmed: 'Since this covenant outline, which was used by the Hittites in the 14th and 13th century B.C. . . . had long been familiar in the time of Moses and was geographically within the reach of Yahweh's people . . . we are justified in assuming that a primordial form of the Decalogue, as the tradition asserts (Exod. xxxiv 27f.; xxiv 4, 7, 12; xx 1), had in fact arisen in the Mosaic period through the use of this treaty form.'[38] This being so then it may be confirmed, he argues, that the Exodus and Sinai traditions were connected from the beginning: 'We may conclude, therefore, that the traditions of the deliverance from Egypt and of the events on Sinai were connected at a very early date under the influence of an old covenant-form going back to the pre-Mosaic period. This is true of the earliest stages of the growth of Israel's tradition and not simply of the later period of

[36] Ibid., 54.   [37] Ibid., 64.   [38] Ibid., 145.

literary fixation, and is the reason for the union of history and law which is characteristic of the Old Testament.'[39]

But Beyerlin pursues this conclusion further and specifies precisely the historical situation as well as the location where the two traditions were united. This took place, he maintains, at Kadesh to which the groups that escaped from Egypt journeyed (cf. Exod. 15–18; Judg. 11:16f.) and where they were based for a considerable period of time (cf. Exod. 16:35; Deut. 1:46; 5:25). Since, according to Deuteronomy 1:2, Sinai/Horeb was eleven days' journey from Kadesh and since it may be identified, as many scholars believe, with the sacred mountain which is later attested as a place of pilgrimage for the Nabataeans, Beyerlin believes that the groups which had escaped from bondage in Egypt went to Sinai/Horeb on a pilgrimage from Kadesh. From Exodus 18:13–27 he deduces that the judicial and social organization of the people of Yahweh was instituted at Kadesh, and he regards it equally probable that 'the basic ordinance of the covenant with Yahweh, the *Decalogue*, may have been first composed in this area'.[40] He concludes: 'The community of those who had experienced Yahweh's saving activity in the deliverance from Egypt and had pledged themselves to obey him understood their tie with Yahweh on the analogy of a vassal-covenant. The same treaty-form which the Hittite kings had used to make their covenant-will law now became the vehicle for expressing something quite new and unique—the majestic revelation of the nature and will of the God of Sinai. . . . The historical prologue of the Decalogue reminded the Yahwistic community of Yahweh's saving-act in delivering them from Egypt and their corresponding obligation of gratitude and obedience; the Ten Commandments themselves contained the demands of the covenant-God.'[41]

We began this chapter with a brief summary of the views of Weiser who argues that the Exodus and Sinai traditions, far from being originally independent of one another as von Rad and others have maintained, were interrelated within the context of one and the same cultic festival in early Israel, a recurring restival of the renewal of the covenant. It is clear that the works of Mendenhall and Beyerlin, whose views in this respect are supported by many others, lend considerable weight to Weiser's thesis, both with

[39] Ibid., 169f. [40] Ibid., 146. [41] Ibid., 146.

regard to the unity of the two traditions and their common cultic *Sitz im Leben*. Furthermore, both Mendenhall and Beyerlin have drawn important conclusions concerning the origins of the Israelite community and the historical connection between the actual events of Exodus and Sinai. But can the arguments adduced by these scholars from the Hittite treaties be sustained?

IV

We may begin by observing that it remains a matter of considerable dispute whether the Decalogue, so important for the views of both Mendenhall and Beyerlin, can in fact be assigned to the early period in Israel's history to which they attribute it.[42] It is also questionable whether it originated within a cultic context, as Beyerlin in particular, following the view of some earlier scholars, has contended.[43] But even if it is accepted that it belonged to the earliest Sinaitic tradition, does it in itself, or when taken together with other material in the Sinai pericope in Exodus 19–24, display the structure of the Hittite vassal treaties of the late Bronze Age and thus warrant the conclusion that the Exodus tradition was interrelated with the Sinai covenant tradition from the very beginning of Israel's existence as the people of Yahweh?

In this connection attention must be drawn to D. J. McCarthy's important work *Treaty and Covenant* which was published in 1963 some years after the studies of both Mendenhall and Beyerlin. It is beyond the scope of our present task to present a full account of McCarthy's work in which he investigates, in addition to the Hittite treaties on which Mendenhall and Beyerlin concentrated, treaty material deriving from earlier and later periods than the Hittite texts, in particular treaty documents of the Assyrian empire of the first millennium B.C. All that need concern us here is McCarthy's conclusions with regard to the view that the earliest

[42] For a recent discussion see J. J. Stamm and M. E. Andrew, *The Ten Commandments in Recent Research*, London 1967; E. Nielsen, *The Ten Commandments in New Perspective*, London 1968.

[43] Cf. E. Nielsen, op. cit., for a recent non-cultic interpretation of the origin of the Decalogue. E. Gerstenberger, *Wesen und Herkunft des 'Apodiktischen Rechts'*, *WMANT* 20 (Neukirchen 1965), has shown that Alt's view of a cultic origin for the apodictic form is untenable and argues that it originated within the context of clan or family instruction, whilst agreeing, however, that the form was also used in the cult.

Sinai covenant tradition is modelled on the Hittite treaty-form.[44]

Already in the introduction to his study he makes an observation of fundamental importance and far-reaching consequences for the use of the treaties in investigating the nature and form of the Sinai covenant material in the Old Testament. He points out, in effect, that whilst all treaties can be classified as covenants, not all covenants were made or expressed in the same manner and with the same structure as the treaties. In other words, there was more than one form of covenant and 'only on the assumption that all covenant must reflect the treaty-form can one proceed from the verification of the fact of a covenant to *the* covenant form'.[45] This means that just because the Old Testament speaks of a covenant between Yahweh and Israel, it does not follow automatically that this covenant was modelled on the international vassal treaty-form of the ancient Near East. It is because Mendenhall and others appear to assume that all covenants were formulated according to the pattern of the treaties that they believe the Decalogue to be in *the* covenant (treaty) form and, having found what they believe to be elements of that form in the Decalogue, have to explain 'how so much of the form—witnesses, curses and blessings, oath—can have been omitted from the text'.[46] McCarthy stresses that the question must be whether the Biblical texts do in fact reflect the structure of the treaties with sufficient fullness to warrant the conclusion that they are dependent with regard to form upon such treaties.

But what were the essential and constant elements of the treaty-form in the ancient Near East? As we have already noted, McCarthy investigates treaty texts deriving not only from the archives of the Hittite empire of the late Bronze Age but also from earlier and later periods. He demonstrates the various differences between treaties from different periods and places. For example, he shows that the historical prologue, so central to the views of Mendenhall and Beyerlin concerning the relationship between the Exodus and covenant traditions, is peculiar to the Hittite treaties and is not found, except for only one exception, in treaties from elsewhere.[47] Another difference is that the treaties from Assyria place great

---

[44] *Treaty and Covenant*, 152–67.   [45] Ibid., 5.   [46] Ibid., 6.

[47] The exception is the Abba-An treaty, probably from the first half of the seventeenth century B.C., which contains a section devoted to the history of what went before the granting of the treaty. Cf. D. J. McCarthy, op. cit., 51ff.

emphasis on the curses, of which they contain long lists, whilst the earlier Hittite texts contain only short and generalized blessings and curses formulae. But in spite of many variations McCarthy argues that there is a fundamental unity in the treaties as a whole: 'Everywhere the basic elements are the same: the provisions are imposed under oath and placed under the sanction of the divine witnesses invoked. And this divine guardianship is invariably made more vivid through the curses which represent (and effect) the dreadful fate of an eventual transgressor. Hence the essential elements of the form: stipulations, the god lists or invocations, and the curse formulae which are invariably found in the treaties from Eannatum of Lagash to Esarhaddon of Assyria.'[48]

On the basis of his detailed investigation of these vassal treaties McCarthy turns to the Old Testament itself to determine whether it contains material which exemplifies the treaty-form with sufficient fullness. He finds clear evidence of the use of this form in the central discourse in Deuteronomy (Deut. 5–28) and of its influence upon other Deuteronomic passages as well as upon Joshua 24 and I Samuel 12. But these passages all belong, at least as they now stand, to a relatively late period in Israel's history, and the question most important for our own investigation is whether the earlier covenant narrative in Exodus 19–24, 32–4 exhibits the treaty-form, thus enabling us to conclude that, as in later literature such as Deuteronomy, history and law converge in the oldest presentation of the Sinai covenant.

From his examination of Exodus 19–24, 32–4 McCarthy concludes that the Sinai covenant as here presented does not exhibit the treaty-form.[49] He acknowledges that the pericope in Exodus 19–24 as it lies before us does resemble much of the treaty-form: there is an introduction comprising parenetic and historical material (Exod. 19), a proclamation of law (Exod. 20:1–23:19), promises of blessing and threats of curses (Exod. 23: 20–33), and ceremonies to ratify the covenant (Exod. 24:1–11). He shows, however, that a more critical investigation of the pericope reveals that such an initial impression cannot be sustained.

Firstly, McCarthy argues that Exodus 19 does not constitute a historical prologue to the covenant after the analogy of the prologue in the Hittite treaties.[50] The only reference to history is

---

[48] Ibid., 80. That is, before the middle of the third millennium B.C. down to the middle of the first millennium B.C.
[49] See his discussion in ibid., 162–7.   [50] Ibid., 155ff.

in *v.* 4, but this verse belongs to a passage (Exod. 19:3b–8) which from the point of view of style, literary character, and the proper sequence of events must be regarded as a secondary insertion into the chapter and not an original part of the Sinai narrative. However, even if it does belong to the original narrative, one verse of history is hardly sufficient to give a historical character to the introduction to the Sinai events in this chapter as a whole. The character of this introduction is of a very different nature from the historical prologue in the Hittite treaties. It is concerned primarily with Yahweh's theophany with its accompanying awful manifestations which evoke the fear and respect of the people on the basis of which their obedience to the divine will contained in the ensuing covenant stipulations can be demanded.

Secondly, McCarthy argues that the promises in Exodus 23:20ff. are not related to the covenant law set out in the previous chapters in Exodus. These promises are not concerned with invoking obedience to the law but seek to encourage obedience to the angel who is to lead the people into the promised land. Promises of divine help in the settlement 'are not in place in the midst of the Sinai events well before the problem of the conquest has been broached'.[51] It is argued that they were attached to the Book of the Covenant (20:22–23:19) before it was inserted into the Sinai pericope at a secondary stage in its development. It is concluded that the original narrative did not include blessings and curses formulae. In this respect also, therefore, the original Sinai tradition does not reflect the vassal treaty-form of which such formulae were an indispensable part. As in the case of the introduction to the covenant in Exodus 19, so here, McCarthy argues, 'the simple manifestation of His (Yahweh's) presence was enough to prove what He could do, to make clear that His will was absolute and not to be violated with impunity'.[52]

Finally, McCarthy argues that the manner of ratifying the covenant by the rites referred to in Exodus 24:1–11 is foreign to the treaties. In Exodus 24:9–11 the ratification of the covenant is the ceremonial meal shared by Moses and the representatives of Israel with Yahweh. As such it symbolizes the 'community' between Yahweh and his people. McCarthy sees 'a certain psychological justness about this',[53] for coming as it did after the theophany with its terrifying manifestations it would have reassured

---

[51] See his discussion in ibid., 154.
[52] Ibid., 157.   [53] Ibid., 162.

the people that 'this mighty God was friendly ... that He had not come to destroy them'.[54] As a means of ratifying a covenant such a rite points to a background in Bedouin culture where it would have been used as a means of taking the weaker into the family of the stronger, 'a reassuring gesture on the part of the superior toward the inferior and not a pledge by the latter'.[55] But, McCarthy concludes, 'the ratification of alliance by rite rather than by a contract based on an oath, and the gesture of superior to inferior rather than vice versa, these things are strangers to the treaty tradition'.[56] The same is also true, he continues, of the alternative ratification rite described in Exodus 24:3–8, the communion sacrifice and the blood rite. They are analogous to the treaties in so far as such rites, like the treaties themselves, seek to produce brotherhood and fellowship. 'But in the treaties, at least among the Hittites, it is the word which effects the desired end; at Sinai it is sacrifice.'[57]

This brings us to the question of the Decalogue. Does it exhibit the treaty-form, as both Mendenhall and Beyerlin have contended? Once again McCarthy argues compellingly that this is not the case. Firstly, he points to the fact that a fundamental element of the treaty-form is entirely lacking in the Decalogue: there are no curse or blessing formulae. Beyerlin, as we have seen, acknow-ledges the difficulty this raises for any attempt to correlate the form of the Decalogue with that of the treaties but argues that the commandments themselves as apodictic formulations setting forth categorical prohibitions are by their very nature absolute and *ipso facto* the most powerful sanctions. But, as McCarthy correctly states, any law, whether apodictic or conditional, implies (or states) a sanction. The point is that the curses and blessings seem to have been an essential member of the treaty-form.[58] After all, the Hittite suzerains intended their stipulations, many of which are apodictic in form, to be taken seriously and yet also and invariably included alongside them in their treaties such curse-blessing formulae.

What of the historical statement at the beginning of the Deca-logue ('I am Yahweh your God who brought you forth from the land of Egypt, out of the house of bondage'), which is regarded by Mendenhall and Beyerlin as a historical prologue after the analogy of the historical prologue to the Hittite treaties? Firstly, there are

[54] Ibid., 162.   [55] Ibid., 162.   [56] Ibid., 162.   [57] Ibid., 163.
[58] See McCarthy's comments, ibid., 159, n. 13.

some grounds for believing that this clause was not an original part of the Decalogue; not a few commentators regard it as a secondary addition.[59] But even if it was an original part of the Decalogue, it is not a historical prologue in the strict sense of that found in the Hittite treaties.[60] In the latter the purpose of the prologue is persuasion, that is, to evoke the proper attitude and response of the vassal towards the suzerain; it does not centre on defining who the suzerain is. In the Decalogue, on the other hand, the introductory sentence serves to designate the speaker and is better understood, McCarthy argues, as a continuation of the theophany. It is, in brief, 'less concerned with what happened than with who did it.'[61]

For these reasons the theory that the earliest Sinai covenant tradition was modelled on the form of Hittite suzerainty treaties must be rejected. At best it seems likely that the treaty-form exemplified in treaties from Assyria in the middle of the first millennium B.C. has influenced the presentation of the covenant in the Deuteronomic and related literature. But this is a late development and quite unknown to the earlier material contained in the Sinai pericope in Exodus 19–24 (JE). This in turn means that the close interrelationship drawn recently by scholars on the basis of these Hittite treaties between the Exodus and Sinai traditions in their earliest history cannot be sustained.

This does not mean, however, that there was no connection of any kind between the two traditions in question, but only that the argument in favour of a relationship between them adduced from the alleged parallels between the Sinai covenant formulations and the Hittite treaties does not carry conviction. In the following chapter we shall see that other arguments are at hand for believing that the two traditions were associated with each other from the outset.

[59] Cf. E. Gerstenberger, op. cit., 57ff.; J. J. Stamm and M. E. Andrew, op. cit., 46; E. Nielson, op. cit., 86.

[60] Cf. D. J. McCarthy, op. cit., 160f. Cf. also G. Fohrer, 'Altes Testament—"Amphiktyonie" und "Bund"?', *Studien zur alttestamentlichen Theologie und Geschichte*, BZAW 115 (Berlin 1969), 107ff.

[61] D. J. McCarthy, *Treaty and Covenant*, 160.

3

Observations, Suggestions and Conclusions

In view of the survey and discussion in the foregoing chapters it would appear that the debate on the problem with which we are concerned has reached something of an *impasse*. Neither the arguments of von Rad and others that the Exodus and Sinai traditions were originally independent of each other in early Israel nor the case advanced against such a view on the basis of Hittite vassal treaties are convincing. Accordingly, further research is necessary into the problem on hand to see if any fresh insights are forthcoming which might suggest a possible solution to it. Various questions arise for consideration and it is with these that we shall be concerned in what follows. What was the original basis and content of the Sinai tradition in Exodus 19ff.? Did it embody from the beginning the belief that a covenant was made between God and Israel at Sinai? Or was the original basis of this tradition the theophany of Yahweh at Sinai? What was the place of Moses in the earliest Exodus and Sinai traditions? Also of fundamental importance is the question whether Yahweh was associated with these traditions from the outset or only secondarily associated with them.

I

We begin with some remarks on the bondage and Exodus. No one today seriously questions that there was a bondage and Exodus. In its basic outlines as well as in a number of details the story of the enslavement of Israel's ancestors in Egypt accords with much that we know of conditions and features of life in the Nile delta region in the latter part of the second millennium B.C.[1] For example, the migration of bedouin (*Shasu*)[2] to this region and their presence there is amply attested in Egyptian texts of this period and earlier.[3] We know also that a class of people called '*pr.w (apiru)* (this word is probably though not certainly to be identified with '*ibrim* 'Hebrews') appear repeatedly as state slaves in documents from the nineteenth and twentieth dynasties. Of particular interest is the fact that during the reign of Rameses II (*ca.* 1290–1224 B.C.) such '*pr.w* appear to have been engaged in building operations. The record in Exodus 1:11, the authenticity of which need not be questioned,[4] according to which Israel's enslaved ancestors 'built for Pharaoh store cities, Pithom and Rameses' is clearly compatible with this, though this does not mean that this verse refers to the same group of slaves. Furthermore, this same verse is widely regarded by scholars as pointing to the first half of the thirteenth century B.C. as the period of the bondage and Exodus.

But if the period of the bondage and Exodus seems relatively clear, the actual nature of the Exodus event itself is very obscure and, we may add, will probably forever remain so. The narrative in Exodus 1–15 describes how a series of plagues visited upon Egypt failed to force Pharaoh to let the Hebrews go free, until the final plague killed the first-born children of the Egyptians, after which Pharaoh hastened the Israelites away. Subsequently, however, we are told that he regretted this and sent some troops in pursuit, a pursuit which ended in the destruction of these troops in the sea (Exod. 14:15). As it now stands there seems little doubt that this narrative has been strongly influenced by the Passover festival (cf.

[1] For a recent and excellent discussion see esp. S. Herrmann, *Israels Aufenthalt in Ägypten*, Stuttgarter Bibelstudien 40, Stuttgart 1970, where also further extensive bibliography is provided.

[2] Cf. R. Giveon, 'The Shosu of Egyptian Sources and the Exodus', in *Fourth World Congress of Jewish Studies*, vol. I (Jerusalem 1967), 193–6. On the tantalizing but not to be overpressed mention of the 'land of the Shasu Yhwɛ' in inscriptions from Soleb see S. Herrmann, 'Der Name Jhwɛ in den Inschriften von Soleb. Prinzipielle Erwägungen', *Fourth World Congress of Jewish Studies*, vol. I, 213–16 and R. de Vaux, *Histoire Ancienne D'Israël*, Paris 1971, 316f.

[3] Cf. S. Herrmann, *Israels Aufenthalt in Ägypten*, 19ff.

[4] D. B. Redford, 'Exodus i 11', *VT* 13 (1963), 401–18 argues that the topographical information here supplied is late and unreliable. Against this, however, see the discussion by W. Helck, '*Tkw* und die Ramses-Stadt', *VT* 15 (1965), 35–48.

Exod. 11–13) and indeed J. Pedersen has presented the view that Exodus 1–15 was actually the cult-legend of that festival, the climax of which was the destruction of the Egyptians in the sea.[5] But as Noth has pointed out,[6] the destruction of the Egyptians in the sea (Exod. 14) follows the Passover celebration (Exod. 11–12) which would surely have formed the climax to and conclusion of a cultic legend such as is proposed by Pedersen. That is to say, the Passover night, though on the face of it constituting the final plague visited upon the Egyptians, as the result of which they not only permit but compel Israel to depart (Exod. 12:29ff.), is followed by a renewed threat to Israel (Exod. 14:5ff.) by the Egyptian forces who are then destroyed. Noth himself argues that the destruction of the Egyptians in the sea constitutes the real nucleus of the Exodus tradition. He believes that the Passover motif came in at a secondary stage and that the plagues narrative was prompted by and developed on the basis of the Passover tradition.[7] But this forces him to conclude that the narrative of the events at the sea comes unexpectedly and serves within its present context only as a 'postlude'.[8]

A much more acceptable case has been advanced by G. W. Coats who has demonstrated that the Reed Sea motif is not the nucleus of the Exodus theme but rather the beginning of the theme of Yahweh's help to the Israelites in the wilderness; as far as the tradition of the destruction at the sea is concerned, the Exodus is presupposed and 'The contact between the Reed Sea motif and the Exodus theme shows simply that the Wilderness theme is not independent of the Exodus theme'.[9] In another short study Coats points to the ancient tradition of an escape from Egypt by stealth with spoil (cf. Exod. 3:21f.; 11:2f.; 12:35f.; Ps. 105:37)[10] and argues that it constitutes an alternative climax for the Exodus theme and a

[5] J. Pedersen, 'Passahfest und Passahlegende', *ZAW* 52 (1934), 161–75 and 'The Crossing of the Reed Sea and the Paschal Legend', in *Israel: Its Life and Culture*, III–IV, Oxford and Copenhagen 1940, Additional Note I, 728–37.

[6] M. Noth, *ÜG*, 71f.   [7] M. Noth, ibid., 70ff.

[8] M. Noth, *Exodus*, 104.

[9] G. W. Coats, 'The traditio-historical character of the Reed Sea motif', *VT* 17 (1967), 265.

[10] Cf. *ÜG*. Fohrer, *Überlieferung und Geschichte des Exodus*, BZAW 91 (Berlin 1964), 82; M. Noth, *Exodus*, 93. Both these scholars regard the motif describing spoil taken from the Egyptians as a subsidiary theme in the Exodus traditions. Coats argues persuasively that it cannot be relegated to such a subordinate position.

much more suitable prelude to the description of the events at the sea.[11] He draws attention to Exodus 10:28f. which appears to bring the plague cycle of stories to a conclusion: the plagues have apparently not succeeded in evoking the desired response from Pharaoh and all further negotiations between Moses and Pharaoh are broken off. Coats then argues that such a termination of negotiations between Moses and Pharaoh may originally have formed the immediate background for a secret escape by the Israelites (further negotiations were impossible and would in any case be to no avail) and that such a secret escape would then readily explain Pharaoh's subsequent pursuit of the Israelites in flight and the destruction of the Egyptians in the sea. Thus Coats is able to conclude: '. . . the tradition of a secret escape with spoil constitutes an alternative climax for the Exodus theme (in addition to the Passover narrative), a proper sequence for at least one facet of the plague traditions, and the description of the Exodus event presupposed in the Reed Sea tradition.'[12]

Of the great antiquity of such a tradition of escape by stealth and its sequel there can be little doubt. That it antedates the tradition centring on the Passover, in which it is now embedded but with which it is not congruous, seems probable; it is unlikely that it could have arisen after the emergence and formulation of the Passover motif which now dominates the bondage-Exodus narrative as a whole. To conclude that it affords us an authentic memory of the actual course of events (only in broad outline of course) of the escape from Egypt would be to go too far, though it might certainly be claimed that in its basic form it offers a credible story.[13] But so complex is the Exodus tradition, presented in Exodus 1–15, that we shall probably never know just what did happen. What we do know, however, is that Israel looked back upon the Exodus as a decisive act of God on her behalf and the belief that 'Yahweh brought Israel forth from the land of Egypt' came to be one of the fundamental tenets of her faith.

More crucial for our present purposes, however, is the question of the relationship between Yahweh and the Exodus tradition: did he belong to this tradition from the beginning or was he associated with it only at a secondary stage in its history and development?

[11] G. W. Coats, 'Despoiling the Egyptians', *VT* 18 (1968), 450–7.
[12] Ibid., 457.
[13] For a discussion as well as a modern incident of such an escape by flight see R. de Vaux, op. cit., 352.

So central and so ancient is the confession that Yahweh delivered
Israel from Egypt, and so very much is it the *sine qua non* of
Israel's faith as presented in the Old Testament, that few commentators have doubted that Yahweh belonged to the Exodus
tradition from the outset or that he was in fact attributed with the
deliverance from bondage from the beginning. One notable
exception to this, as we have seen, is Noth who believes that the
clans who escaped from Egypt identified the God who delivered
them from bondage with Yahweh only at a later time in their
history, that is, when they became part of Israel and began to
worship Yahweh the God of Israel after their settlement in the
land of Canaan.[14] Such a view is difficult if not impossible to
disprove. It in no way conflicts with the belief in the great importance of the Exodus for Israel's faith, for Noth of course does
not question the antiquity of the Yahweh-Exodus relationship; on
the contrary, he himself believes the confession that 'Yahweh
brought Israel forth from the land of Egypt' to be the very essence
of Israel's faith and indeed, as we have seen, the nucleus of the
Pentateuchal tradition as a whole. But if such a view is impossible
to disprove, the balance of probability surely lies heavily against
it and in favour of the view that the miracle of the Exodus was
attributed to Yahweh from the outset, that means already in
the wilderness, and not just at a later time in the post-settlement
period.

Noth's view clearly presupposes that before their entry into the
land of Canaan and their absorption into the tribes which subsequently made up Israel, the Exodus group attributed their
miraculous deliverance to some other god. But as far as I am aware
he nowhere elucidates this or attempts to determine the identity of
this god. If, however, it had been some other god who was
initially believed to have delivered the slaves from bondage, it may
justly be asked whether that god would have disappeared so
completely from the scene as Noth's suggestion seems to imply.
Is it likely that that god would have been so easily forgotten by
those who worshipped him as their champion against the Egyptian
might? But perhaps more to the point, in the absence of any hint
of this presumed erstwhile god of the Exodus, does it not seem very
likely that the best, one may indeed plausibly claim, the only,
candidate for the role of the saving God is Yahweh who, as we
have reason to believe,[15] was the God of Sinai in the southern

[14] M. Noth, *The History of Israel*, 136.   [15] See below, 62f.

desert and was worshipped by nomadic or semi-nomadic groups
throughout that region? It would appear that Noth is really led to
his conclusion simply because of the particular manner in which
he believes Israel and her faith to have originated and developed.
But short of being sceptical, there is no substantial reason for
doubting that those who escaped from bondage in Egypt
believed themselves from the outset to have been delivered by
Yahweh. We may conclude therefore that Yahweh was associated with the Exodus tradition from the very beginning and
that any suggestion that he was related to it only at a secondary
stage in the development of the Exodus tradition is highly
questionable.

One further important question must here be briefly considered,
the question of the place of Moses in the bondage-Exodus
traditions. Did he belong originally to these traditions or has he
been associated with them only at a secondary stage in their
transmission and development?

There can be no doubt that in these traditions as we now have
them in Exodus 1–15 the figure of Moses is of supreme importance
and this together with other considerations, such as for example
his Egyptian name,[16] has led most scholars to accept that however
much his originality in other Pentateuchal traditions may be
questioned he was from the beginning indispensably integral to
the bondage-Exodus complex of traditions. Most scholars still
believe that however obscure the events of bondage and Exodus
may be, there are no sound grounds for doubting that Moses in
some way played a leading role in them.

The most notable recent exception to this is Noth who has
argued that Moses was only secondarily associated with the
bondage-Exodus traditions and that, in so far as we can discern any
nucleus of historical fact about him, he had nothing to do with the
events underlying these traditions.[17] Noth bases his argument in
this connection on the narrative in Exodus 5:6–19 in which, he
observes, it is not Moses who negotiates with Pharaoh but the
Israelite 'foremen', whilst Moses 'as it is suddenly and surprisingly

[16] The name Moses is derived from the Egyptian *mŝi* 'to beget', 'to
give birth to' and is to be identified with the element *-mose* in theophoric
names such as Thut*mose* which means '(the god) Thut has begotten (him)'.
The short name Moses, that is, without the theophoric element, is also
attested in Egyptian (cf. S. Herrmann, 'Mose', *EvTh* 28 (1968), 303f.
where also further bibliography is provided).

[17] Cf. M. Noth, *ÜG*, 178ff.

revealed in *v.* 20 has in the meantime waited outside!'.[18] Noth
believes that this passage reflects 'a stage in the development of
the tradition in which the figure of Moses had not yet been
inserted into the theme of "the leading forth from Egypt", but
rather the elders of the Israelites still functioned as the spokesmen
over against the Egyptians'.[19] As for the admittedly Egyptian
name of Moses, it does not necessarily indicate that Moses was
ever in Egypt, since in the late Bronze Age, when Syria-Palestine
had long been under Egyptian hegemony, anyone living in that
region could have had an Egyptian name without ever having been
in Egypt.[20]

This argument must be rejected, for the fact that Moses is not
mentioned in this narrative is far from being grounds for such a
conclusion. On the contrary, the very nature of the events described
here offers a satisfactory explanation of his absence from the
narrative, so much so that if he were mentioned in it we could
claim with some justification that his presence was inserted only
secondarily into the story recorded here.

The scene described centres on a situation in which the Egyptian
authorities are taking steps to counter the restlessness of the
Israelite slaves by increasing the difficulties under which they
carry out their labours in making bricks for Pharaoh's building
operations. In such a situation it is to be expected that those
immediately responsible for the supervision of the work in question,
the Egyptian overseers and the Israelite 'foremen' (we observe in
passing, against Noth's conclusion in this connection, that there is
no mention of 'elders' in this narrative) should alone be involved in
the procedure described.[21] They are summoned to Pharaoh's
presence, given the instructions concerning the new conditions
under which the Israelites are to work, and sent out to implement
them. The presence of the Israelite 'foremen' rather than Moses at
this particular point in the bondage narrative is surely singularly
appropriate. The narrative further fills in the background against
which the work of Moses takes place. It is not in itself, contrary to
Noth's understanding of it, a story concerning the negotiations for
the release of the Israelites from bondage but depicts the further
aggravation of Israel's hardship in bondage and so heightens both
the necessity for those negotiations and the role of Moses as

---

[18] Ibid., 76.   [19] Ibid., 76.   [20] Ibid., 178.
[21] Cf. R. Smend, *Yahweh War and Tribal Confederation*, E.T. by M. G.
Rogers, New York–Nashville, 1970, 125.

deliverer.[22] It is true that Exodus 5:6–19 probably does not belong from a literary point of view with the surrounding narrative; it appears to interrupt the connection between the beginning of the chapter and *vv.* 20ff. To that extent any conclusion with regard to the original context of *vv.* 6–19 is an argument from silence. In its present context, however, it has, from the point of view of narrative art, an immediately recognizable function and the possibility cannot be excluded that in its original context it served the same purpose. That is, it is possible that it belonged originally to a sequence of stories concerning the 'charismatic' leadership of Moses, whose role as Israel's champion against the hardship imposed upon them by the Egyptians it serves to heighten and augment. It has certainly all the characteristics of such a story.

Whatever the original context of this narrative was, however, it is no basis on which to argue that Moses was originally absent from the bondage-Exodus traditions. The episode described requires only the presence of Pharaoh, the Egyptian overseers and the Israelite 'foremen'; they alone have a function to perform in the incident described and they alone are essential to it; any mention of Moses would be superfluous.

Furthermore, Noth's assessment of the significance of the Egyptian name of Moses is scarcely admissible. It may be conceded that the Egyptian hegemony of Syria-Palestine would have meant that anyone living in that territory could have had an Egyptian name without ever having been in Egypt itself. It may reasonably be claimed, however, that the chances of this happening would have varied considerably from one place to another. Although Egyptian influence may have been marked in the cities it would have been much less so outside the main centres of population and, of signal importance in the case of Moses, surely much less again in the life of semi-nomadic people (to whom Moses, on Noth's own view, belonged) who lived for only part of the year in the land and even then predominantly in the sparsely populated or indeed unpopulated territory there, which was well away from the main centres of population where the Egyptian influence Noth has in mind would have been largely concentrated. Outside the land and on the desert fringes, semi-nomads cannot be said to have

---

[22] Smend (ibid., 125ff.) draws a pertinent analogy between the position of Moses *vis-à-vis* such a narrative as this and the place of Jeroboam in the narrative of the revolt against Rehoboam in 1 Kgs. 12 as preserved in the LXX.

been under Egyptian hegemony in any real sense of the word. Admittedly this does not eliminate the possibility that Moses could have acquired his name as the son of parents whose semi-nomadic existence led them periodically into Palestine where they chanced to come into contact with Egyptians or Egyptian influence. But given the knowledge that semi-nomads also migrated to the Nile delta it surely seems much more likely that he acquired his Egyptian name because the clan in which he was born migrated frequently to the pasture land in the Nile delta rather than Canaan.

For these reasons Noth's view that Moses was originally unknown to the bondage-Exodus traditions is not compelling. On the contrary, it seems probable that of all the major Pentateuchal traditions it is in this tradition that the figure of Moses is strongest and most original.

II

Let us now turn to the Sinai tradition. Here the issues involved are of no less and perhaps of even greater complexity than those of the Exodus tradition. Nevertheless, it may fairly be claimed that it holds the key to the solution of the problem with which we are concerned and it is therefore of cardinal importance to determine as far as possible the original basis and content of this tradition and its early history in ancient Israel. The *locus classicus* of the Sinai tradition is of course Exodus 19–24 (32–4) and it is with this material that we shall be primarily concerned in the ensuing discussion.

It is unnecessary for our purposes to become involved with the question of the location of mount Sinai. A number of different mountains in several different areas have been advocated over the years.[23] The traditional site, which has its modern advocates, is *Jebul Musa* (the 'mountain of Moses') in the southern part of the Sinai peninsula, though it is difficult to trace the tradition any further back than the fourth century A.D. Several scholars argue the

[23] For a concise survey of the discussion of this problem see J. P. Hyatt, *Exodus*, London 1971, 203ff. I cannot here go into a discussion of the question whether Sinai, Horeb and 'the mountain of God' originally designated more than one mountain. For my own part I believe these names all refer to one and the same mountain.

case for one of the extinct volcanic peaks in north-west Arabia, chiefly because of the volcanic imagery in the account of the theophany in Exodus 19.[24] Some others have attempted to locate it in the region of Kadesh, thus eliminating the break which is believed to exist between the so-called Kadesh cycle of stories in Exodus 15:22–18:27 and the Sinai pericope which follows it, a break which, as we have seen, has been taken by many scholars as evidence of the late insertion of the Sinai story into an earlier narrative relating a journey from Egypt after the Exodus to Kadesh. So far no consensus of opinion has been reached on this question of the location of Sinai, through further research into the 'itineraries' of the Israelites in the wilderness described in Exodus 15ff., Numbers 33 and elsewhere in the Old Testament may eventually lead to further clarification.

One further preliminary but crucially important observation must here be made. There is not a little evidence in the Old Testament which points to an intimate connection between Yahweh and Sinai and indicates that from ancient times he was regarded as the God of Sinai. Several old poetic texts (Deut. 33:2, 26; Judg. 5:4–5; Ps. 68:8–9; Hab. 3:3–4) point to and confirm the ancient belief that Yahweh's (original) home was in the region south of the land of Canaan. These texts mention several places from which Yahweh 'comes'—Sinai, Seir, Paran, the plains of Edom, Teman—but of these it is widely agreed that Sinai gives the impression of the greatest antiquity. Outside the Pentateuch and independently of its major literary sources, Sinai is mentioned only in Deuteronomy 33:2, Judges 5:5 and Psalm 68:9. Furthermore, the enigmatic expression *zē sīnāy* in Judges 5:5 and Psalm 68:9 is probably to be understood as designating Yahweh as 'the One (i.e. Lord) of Sinai'.[25] Taken together with all that we now

---

[24] It is, however, hazardous to attach too much significance to this imagery in any attempt to determine the possible location of Sinai, since such imagery was probably one of the conventional ways of describing theophanies in the ancient Near East. See the comments by M. Noth, *Exodus*, 159f. Cf. the observations by T. W. Mann, 'The Pillar of Cloud in the Reed Sea Narrative', *JBL* 90 (1971), 15ff.

[25] On this see, e.g., W. F. Albright, 'The Names Shaddai and Abram', *JBL* 54 (1935), 204; 'The Song of Deborah in the Light of Archaeology', *BASOR* 62 (1936), 30. Against such an understanding of the expression see H. Birkeland, 'Hebrew *Zāe* and Arabic *Ḏū*', *StTh* 2 (1948), 201–2. But against Birkeland see J. M. Allegro, 'Uses of the Semitic demonstrative element Z in Hebrew', *VT* 5 (1955), 309–12.

know about the attachment of gods to sacred mountains in ancient Near Eastern religions,[26] it seems clear that there was from ancient times a special relationship between Yahweh and mount Sinai, a relationship which was already in existence before the Exodus from Egypt and the emergence of Israel.

Broadly speaking the material presented in the Sinai pericope in Exodus 19:1–24:11 falls into three divisions: the theophany in chapter 19, the laws in 20:1–23:19 (the Decalogue and 'the book of the covenant') together with a short passage concerning the journey to the promised land and warnings against the danger of apostasy there (23:20–33), and finally a record of the performance of certain rites (24:1–11). We have already seen that these divisions in the pericope have been regarded by the majority of scholars as witnessing to a ceremony of covenant making, though the view advanced recently by some that the pericope exhibits the form of ancient Near Eastern vassal treaties cannot be sustained. Nevertheless, it remains true that as it now lies before us the narrative does purport to describe a ceremony of covenant making at Sinai: Yahweh manifests himself, the divine law is proclaimed by Moses, and the covenant is ratified.

Within the framework of this pericope Yahweh's theophany and the making of the covenant between him and Israel are closely interrelated. The question arises, however, whether these two elements were constituent parts of the Sinai tradition from the beginning. We have seen that Noth, for example, believes that the theophany constituted the nucleus of this tradition and that the combination of this original theophany tradition with the covenant came about only at a later time, specifically as the result of the theophany tradition having been transmitted within the context of a recurring covenant renewal festival of the Israelite amphictyony in the land of Canaan. The question therefore arises of the antiquity of these two constituents of the Sinai pericope in Exodus 19:1–24:11.

Let us begin with the question of the covenant. Two passages within the pericope arise for consideration in this connection, for it is largely if not exclusively on the basis of them that the view that there was a covenant between Yahweh and Israel at Sinai rests. The passages in question are Exodus 19:3b–8 and 24:1–11. The former, as we have seen, is a secondary insertion into the chapter and, although the source from which it derives is disputed, the

[26] Cf. R. E. Clements, *God and Temple*, Oxford 1965, 1ff., 19ff.

balance of probability is that it is the work of a Deuteronomic redactor.[27] This being so, it obviously cannot be the basis for an assessment of the nature of the earliest Sinai tradition. But the second passage is of crucial importance, for the rites there described have been understood by most modern commentators to constitute a ceremony of ratifying a covenant between Yahweh and Israel. Furthermore, the material in these verses is widely regarded as being of very ancient origin and thus as evidence for the antiquity of the covenant.

Before directing our attention to this passage one preliminary question must be clarified, viz. what is a covenant? A very considerable amount has been written on this subject in recent years and it remains a matter of controversy. It is beyond the scope of our task here to concern ourselves with a discussion of the very complex issues involved in this problem.[28] Some brief comments will suffice for our purposes, though the point of view adopted here would not be shared by some other Old Testament scholars.

The etymology of the Old Testament word *berîth*, 'covenant', is obscure, but those explanations of it have gained most acceptance which understand it as designating a mutual agreement or arrangement between two (or more) parties.[29] Wherever it occurs in the Old Testament in a secular usage, *berîth* designates an arrangement or contract between two (or more) parties and involves the mutual acceptance of obligations which are either stated or implied in the texts in question.[30] For example, Abraham and

[27] The similarity between the phraseology of *v.* 5 and Deut. 7:6; 14:2; 26:18 is especially striking. See the impressive list of parallels or close similarities between this passage and the Deuteronomic literature in B. Baentsch, *Exodus-Leviticus-Numeri*, Göttingen 1903, 171. A number of commentators ascribe the passage to E though not a few of them also believe it to have been worked over by a Deuteronomic editor.

[28] For a recent survey with an extensive bibliography see D. J. McCarthy, *Old Testament Covenant: A Survey of Current Opinion*, Oxford 1972.

[29] The most favoured etymologies are: (1) that the word derives from *bārāh* = 'to eat', hence to make a covenant by eating a common meal; (2) that it is from an Accadian work *birtu* = 'fetter', 'bond', hence a covenant is the creation of a 'bond' between two or more parties; (3) that is from another Accadian word *birit* = 'between', hence to make a covenant is to 'cut (*kārath*) between' two or more parties.

[30] This understanding of covenant is that presented by G. Quell in his brief study of covenant in G. Kittel's *Theological Dictionary of the New Testament*, II, Grand Rapids 1964, 106ff. (first published in German in 1935).

Abimelech have a dispute about a well which they resolve by making a covenant, a 'pact' as the New English Bible renders it (Gen. 21:25ff.). Laban and Jacob make a covenant, an agreement, about the former's daughters who are Jacob's wives (Gen. 31:43ff.). We read of a covenant between David and Jonathan concerning what each would do in the event of the death of Saul (1 Sam. 23:14ff.). On the political level, Solomon and Hiram of Tyre make a covenant, a treaty (1 Kgs. 5:12), whilst at a later time a greatly weakened Israel makes a covenant with Assyria (cf. Hos. 12:1). Such examples as these also indicate that a covenant could be between equals or between a superior partner and an inferior.

It is clear that when applied to the relationship between Israel and Yahweh such an understanding of $b^e r\hat{\imath}th$ is problematic, for it suggests on the one hand that Israel could earn Yahweh's grace and favour, and on the other hand that God himself was bound to a contract with Israel. Against this, the Old Testament always portrays a marked element of grace in the notion and interpretation of the covenant between Yahweh and Israel. Not surprisingly, therefore, a number of scholars have rejected such an understanding of covenant as that outlined above, at least with regard to the covenant between Yahweh and Israel, and have attempted instead to interpret $b^e r\hat{\imath}th$ as the giving of a solemn promise or oath,[31] or alternatively, as the establishing of a relationship between two parties by the acceptance of obligations by one of the parties or the imposition of such obligations by one of the parties upon the other.[32] Thus the Sinai covenant, according to the former of these two views, means that Yahweh made a solemn promise or oath to

[31] Cf. J. Begrich, 'Berit. Ein Beitrag zur Erfassung einer alttestamentlichen Denkform', *ZAW* 60 (1944), 1–11. Begrich distinguishes between two different concepts of covenant: one was promissory and this was what the Sinai covenant originally was; the other was current among the Canaanites and involved contract and legal obligation. After the settlement, it is argued, the latter eventually replaced the older Israelite understanding of covenant. More recently, A. Jepsen, 'Berith. Ein Beitrag zur Theologie der Exilszeit', in *Verbannung und Heimkehr*, Festschrift for W. Rudolph, Tübingen 1961, 161–80, though criticizing Begrich's work in a number of matters, also understands Yahweh's covenant with Israel as referring to his giving of his own gracious promise.

[32] For this view see E. Kutsch, 'Gesetz und Gnade. Probleme des alttestamentlichen Bundesbegriffs' *ZAW* 79 (1967), 18–35 and other articles (see bibliography). For comments on Kutsch's views see D. J. McCarthy, *Old Testament Covenant*, 59f.

Israel, or, according to the latter view, that he brought Israel into a relationship with himself which imposed obligations upon Israel but not upon himself. The interpretation of *berîth* as 'promise' is substantiated, it is claimed, by the covenant between Yahweh and Abraham and that between Yahweh and David, both of which involve the solemn promise or oath of God without any obligations being placed upon either of the receiving parties.

But neither of these views is compelling. With regard to the first, that the covenant was Yahweh's promise or oath to Israel, the long process of transmission and development through which the Abrahamic covenant tradition passed in early Israel renders it hazardous to draw any far-reaching conclusions on the basis of it concerning the meaning of *berîth*. Besides, can we really believe that the covenant between God and Abraham involved no obligations upon the latter? There would surely have been the obligation that Abraham and his descendants were to continue to worship the God in question and, since the main feature of the covenant was the promise of land, it is possible that the tithes of the produce of the land and the firstborn of the flocks and herds would have been required by this God as offerings.[33] As for the covenant between Yahweh and David, there are grounds for believing that it also involved certain conditions and obligations on the part of David and his descendants. Once again it would surely be absurd to believe that the Davidic kings were not required to worship Yahweh. Furthermore, Psalm 132:12 seems to make Yahweh's promise to David conditional. In addition, it is possible that the Davidic covenant as a 'ruler covenant' may have involved Israel as a third party upon whom certain obligations were laid, notably the obligation of recognizing the Davidic kings as the only legitimate rulers of Yahweh's people.[34] This also would mean that the Yahweh-David covenant was not as purely promissory as it may first appear. As for the view that the covenant between Yahweh and Israel involved the imposition of obligations upon Israel alone, this also is surely inadmissible. For it seems clear that

[33] Cf. the remarks by R. E. Clements, *Abraham and David: Genesis 15 and its Meaning for Israelite Tradition*, London 1967, 33f.

[34] P. J. Calderone, *Dynastic Oracle and Suzerainty Treaty*, Logos I, Manila 1966, argues that the covenant between Yahweh and David is closely similar to the vassal treaties of Esarhaddon: both were concerned with the question of royal succession, and the function of both was to secure a stable kingdom by ensuring the succession of a particular dynasty.

the Sinai covenant was not understood as merely the imposition of obligations upon Israel, but that it also announced Israel's privileged and elect relationship to Yahweh together with the promise of Yahweh's gift of the land and his continued presence with his people.[35] That is to say, there is little reason to question that Israel regarded the covenant as bilateral, though the Old Testament leaves us in no doubt that this did not involve the belief that Yahweh was an equal partner with Israel. All the indications are that the covenant expressed a relationship between God and Israel involving both law and grace. It was precisely this that gave rise to a major crisis in Israel's faith: how were God's gracious promises to and for Israel to be fulfilled in the face of Israel's rebellion and failure to live in accordance with his righteous will. In the Deuteronomic literature, where the covenant between Yahweh and Israel finds its fullest formulation and presentation, this crisis is the central issue of concern.

We now turn to a consideration of the traditions embodied in Exodus 24:1–11. There can be no doubt that this passage as we now have it describes a rite of covenant ratification: Moses announces 'the words of Yahweh' to the people who pledge themselves to obey; sacrifice and blood rite follow by means of which, it is usually understood, the two parties to the covenant, Yahweh and Israel, are bound together, after which the elders ascend the mountain to eat a meal in the presence of God. But the issue cannot be settled as easily as this suggests, for a closer examination of this passage reveals that it is the work of a redactor who has combined two originally separate units of tradition. The two units in question are (1) *vv.* 9–11 the introduction to which is contained in *vv.* 1–2, and (2) *vv.* 3–8. The latter clearly interrupts the obvious connection between *vv.* 1–2 and 9–11. It is widely maintained that these two originally separate units of tradition are each concerned with a covenant rite; *vv.* 3–8 describing the ratification of the covenant by means of sacrifice and blood rite; *vv.* 9–11 narrating the making of the covenant by means of the eating of a covenant meal, as the phrase in *v.* 11 'they ate and drank' is usually understood. Whilst the majority of commentators agree in isolating these two traditions from each other, there has been no agreement as to which of the Pentateuchal sources they each belong, though it is widely

[35] Even in the international suzerainty treaties drawn up between an overlord and a vassal, the suzerain had clearly certain obligations towards the vassal, e.g., to protect the vassal from attack by an enemy.

acknowledged that they belong to the oldest literary strata of the Pentateuch, J and E. For our present purposes, however, the question of their sources need not concern us.

As to the first of these two passages, there can be no doubt of the great antiquity of the tradition it embodies.[36] This is evidenced not only by the reference to Nadab and Abihu (they are nowhere else referred to in the earliest Pentateuchal documents) but also by the remarkable statement that the representatives of Israel on the mountain 'saw the God of Israel'.[37] The basis for the view that this ancient passage describes a rite of covenant ratification is of course the statement at the end of *v.* 11 'they ate and drank', which is almost universally interpreted as referring to a meal eaten by the representatives of Israel on the mountain in the presence of God. There is ample evidence that the eating of a common meal was a widespread means of covenant ratification in the ancient Near East and in Israel itself (cf. Gen. 26:28ff.; 31:43ff.). The passage does not actually mention the word usually translated 'covenant' (*berîth*). Noth states, however, that 'the fact that God lets the representatives of Israel hold a meal in his presence on the mountain indicates the making of the covenant between God and people'.[38]

That the eating of a meal was employed as a means of ratifying a covenant cannot be questioned. This does not mean, however, that eating and drinking together was *ipso facto* to make a covenant. Sharing a meal presupposed or created a special relationship between those partaking in it, but such a relationship was not necessarily a covenant relationship. A covenant created a special relationship between two parties, but a relationship between two parties did not imply a covenant between them. For example, David and Jonathan formed a close personal relationship with one another, a relationship of mutual trust and affection. But they felt it necessary to make a covenant concerning what they each would do in the event of Saul's death (1 Sam. 24:14ff.). Neither 'table fellowship' nor a deep bond of friendship between two parties can seriously be understood as being synonymous with covenant.

Nor did the eating of a meal in the presence of God necessarily mean or involve the making of a covenant between God and those

---

[36] I hope to publish a more detailed study of Exod. 24:9–11 in the near future.

[37] On the antiquity of this tradition see below, 81.

[38] M. Noth, *Exodus*, 196.

who so ate in his presence. Noth's claim that 'the fact that God lets the representatives of Israel hold a meal in his presence on the mountain indicates the making of the covenant between God and people' certainly cannot be sustained. We note on passing that there is no record of God participating in the eating and drinking referred to in Exodus 24:11. It is obvious of course, as Noth points out,[39] that Yahweh could not have been thought of as participating in a covenant meal in the way that human partners to a covenant did. It is nevertheless to be noted that there is no mention of any part of the meal being offered up sacrificially to God after the manner of the so-called 'communion sacrifice', which would have been a means of God's partaking in the meal, unless it is supposed that the eating and drinking here referred to is to be related to the sacrifices offered in *vv.* 3–8. Since, however, it is widely agreed that *vv.* 3–8 constitute an originally separate unit of tradition from *vv.* 9–11, such a possibility must be excluded.

That a meal eaten in the presence of God was not *ipso facto* a covenant meal may be seen from a glance at the narrative in Exodus 18:1–12. In this narrative we read that after the Exodus the Israelites met with the Midianites led by Moses's father-in-law, Jethro. On hearing of 'all the good Yahweh had done for Israel' Jethro uttered a blessing to Yahweh after which he offered sacrifices and, we are told, together with Aaron and the elders of Israel 'ate bread in the presence of God' (*v.* 12). In this latter respect —the eating of a meal in the presence of God—the procedure is the same as that described in Exodus 24:9–11, but it is obviously inadmissible to describe what takes place at 'the mountain of God' in Exodus 18:1–12 as the ratification of a covenant between Yahweh on the one hand and the Israelites and Midianites on the other. It has been suggested that the passage preserves the memory of the making of a covenant between Israel and the Midianites in which Yahweh was the divine guarantor and witness.[40] But the passage appears to describe nothing more than an act of worship of which the eating of a meal 'before God' was part and a means of rejoicing in the presence of God.[41] In any event, what is described cannot seriously be understood as the making of

[39] Ibid., 196.
[40] Cf. C. H. W. Brekelmans, 'Exodus xviii and the origins of Yahwism in Israel', *OTS* 10 (1954), 215–24; F. C. Fensham, 'Did a Treaty between the Israelites and the Kenites Exist?', *BASOR* 175 (1964), 51–4.
[41] See below, 80.

a covenant between Yahweh and those who worshipped and ate together at 'the mountain of God'. This in turn renders untenable the usual interpretation of Exodus 24:9–11 automatically and exclusively in terms of the ratification of a covenant between Yahweh and Israel; the mere eating of a meal in the presence of God is not synonymous with covenant ratification.

We shall return presently to a further consideration of how the ancient tradition preserved in Exodus 24:9–11 is to be understood. At this point, however, we turn to the other passage which we have isolated from Exodus 24, that is, *vv.* 3–8.

A glance at this passage is sufficient to show that it constitutes a much firmer basis than *vv.* 9–11 in the same chapter for the view that a covenant was made between Yahweh and Israel at Sinai. For in *vv.* 3–8, Moses announces to the people 'the words of Yahweh' and reads to them 'the book of the covenant' to which the people respond with a pledge of obedience, all of which is accompanied by a sacrifice and blood rite binding together, it is usually argued, the two partners to the covenant, Yahweh, represented by the altar on which part of the blood is sprinkled, and Israel on whom also some of the blood is sprinkled. But a closer examination of this passage raises at least the possibility that it is not as firm a basis for such a conclusion as a superficial reading of its suggests.

The passage comprises two distinctive elements: (*a*) the sacrifice and blood rite, and (*b*) the proclamation of 'the words of Yahweh', 'the book of the covenant', together with the people's pledge to obey. As to the former, we need only note that most commentators are agreed that the tradition here preserved is of great antiquity, largely on account of the role of 'the young men of Israel' rather than priests in offering sacrifice (*v.* 5). As to the second, there are reasons for believing that it derives from a late redactor who has worked over an ancient record of a ceremony involving sacrifice and blood rite so as to interpret and present it as having been a covenant ceremony.[42] The proclamation of the covenant terms, 'the words of Yahweh', occurs twice, first in *v.* 3 and again in *v.* 7. In both instances it is the same except only that the apparently oral report of the covenant law in the first is replaced by the reading of 'the book of the covenant' in the second. It has been argued that the first represents the 'preliminary agreement' of the people to the

---

[42] For a recent detailed discussion of these verses see L. Perlitt, *Bundestheologie im Alten Testament*, WMANT 36 (Neukirchen 1969), 190ff.

covenant terms, whilst the second records the 'final obligation'.[43]
But the second proclamation and pledge appears to interrupt the
ritual: the sacrifices are offered and half of the blood is sprinkled
upon the altar; this is followed by the reading of 'the book of the
covenant' and the people's pledge to obey, only after which (*v.* 8) is
the second half of the ritual performed. If, however, the ritual was
the means of ratifying the covenant between both partners then
surely one would expect to find the people's pledge *before* the
performance of the rite and not, somewhat awkwardly as it seems,
in the middle of it. From this point of view the so-called 'preliminary pledge' in *v.* 3 is in a more suitable position: the covenant
law is announced to the people, they pledge their obedience to it
and then the ritual of ratification is performed. But the originality
of *v.* 3 itself is questionable, for in both structure and phraseology
it is strikingly similar to Exodus 19:7–8a which belongs to a passage
already seen to be a secondary (probably Deuteronomic) insertion
into that chapter. The contents of both texts are the same: (*a*)
Moses in the role of mediator between God and the people comes
from his meeting with God and (*b*) reports God's words to the
assembly after which (*c*) the people pledge themselves to obey
God's commands. As to phraseology, here also both texts are
strikingly similar to each other.

Exodus 19:7–8a:

> *And Moses came* and summoned the elders of the people and
> set before then *all these words* which Yahweh had com-
> manded. *And all the people answered together and said: 'All
> that Yahweh has spoken we will do'*.

Exodus 24:3:

> *And Moses came* and told the people *all the words of Yahweh*
> and all the laws. *And all the people answered with one voice
> and said: 'All* the words *which Yahweh has spoken we will do'*.

These striking parallels between these two texts surely indicate
that both derive from the same author and since, as already noted,
Exodus 19:7–8a has all the appearance of having been composed
by a Deuteronomic author so also Exodus 24:3 is to be attributed
to the same source. Furthermore, Exodus 24:7 which, as we have

[43] Cf. M. Noth, *Exodus*, 197f.

already seen, overloads the passage, is itself very similar in phraseology to these other two texts and is therefore also probably from a Deuteronomic redactor. Exodus 24:7:

> And he (Moses) took the book of the covenant and read it to the people. *And they said: 'All that Yahweh has spoken we will do and we will obey'.*

For these reasons it is possible, one may claim probable, that Exodus 24:3 and Exodus 24:7 are redactional. In addition, since *v.* 8 clearly presupposes the contents of these two verses, it also probably owes at least its present form to the same redactor.

What then of the remaining material in Exodus 24:3–8 centring on the sacrifice and blood rite? If this is the original 'layer' of tradition in the passage does it nevertheless describe a covenant ritual? Noth has argued that even with the removal of the clauses about 'the words of Yahweh' the report of the sacrifice and its accompanying blood rite could form a proper account of the making of a covenant.[44] The basis for such an argument is clear: the sprinkling of the blood of the sacrificial victims upon both the altar and the people effects the union between God and Israel which is the object of the covenant. But such an argument is not convincing, as the following observations show.

In the history of the interpretation of this passage attention has often been drawn, following the pioneering work of W. Robertson Smith,[45] to the making of covenants by blood rites in pre-Islamic Arabia. Whilst it is not impossible that evidence from such a source may shed light upon the problem with which we are concerned, it must nevertheless be borne in mind that the material from which such evidence is adduced is considerably far removed in time from the period of Israel's origins. Great caution is therefore necessary in utilizing such material and it is clear that from the point of view of method it is much sounder to attempt to understand the blood rite in Exodus 24:3ff. on the basis of evidence contained elsewhere in the Old Testament itself before resorting to extra-Biblical sources.

Is such evidence forthcoming? In so far as it describes a blood rite in which the blood of sacrificial victims is sprinkled upon the

[44] Ibid., 197.
[45] W. Robertson Smith, *Lectures on the Religion of the Semites*, 3rd ed. by S. A. Cook, London 1927, 314ff.

people generally, the tradition in Exodus 24:3ff. is unique. Nevertheless, apart from this particular aspect of the rite described, a similar 'manipulation' of blood is attested elsewhere in the Pentateuch (Exod. 29:19ff.; Lev. 8:22ff.; 14:1ff.). The first two of these describe the ritual for the installation (the Hebrew expression means literally 'a filling (of the hands)')[46] of Aaron and his sons. A sacrificial victim, a ram, is slaughtered, some of its blood smeared on the right ear, the right thumb and the big toe of the right foot of Aaron and his sons, and the blood is sprinkled (the same word—*zāraq*—is used here as in Exod. 24:6, 8a) upon the altar. Blood is then taken from the altar and, together with anointing oil, is thrown upon the vestments of Aaron and his sons. By these means both Aaron and his sons and their vestments become 'holy' (Exod. 29:1; Lev. 8:30). In essence the rite is the same as that described in Exodus 24:3ff. Yet even though a covenant between Yahweh and the Aaronite priesthood is mentioned elsewhere (cf. Num. 18:19; 25:12, 13), it does not seem at all likely that the rite described in Exodus 29:19ff. and Leviticus 8:22ff. was thought of as inaugurating such a covenant; these texts make no mention whatsoever of a covenant and appear to centre on something quite different. In Leviticus 14 a similar blood rite is described but in this case it is that prescribed for the purification of a man who has had a malignant skin disease. It also has obviously nothing to do with the ratification of a covenant. The rites described in these texts are better understood in terms of consecration and purification. Accordingly, the fact that the blood rite they describe cannot be understood in terms of covenant making surely renders it inadmissible, in the absence of other evidence, to infer without further ado that what is basically the same rite in Exodus 24:3ff., is a rite of covenant ratification.

As to the belief that the altar in Exodus 24:4,6 upon which blood is sprinkled represents God as one of the covenant partners, the same procedure is followed in Exodus 29:19ff. where it seems highly improbable that the altar is to be thought of as representing Yahweh. Indeed, it would appear that the only reason for believing that the altar in Exodus 24:6 represents God, is precisely the prior belief that the rite being performed was a rite of covenant ratification. Without such a presupposition there are no grounds for understanding the significance of the sprinkling of blood on the altar in such a manner. What evidence we possess suggests that

[46] Cf. R. de Vaux, *Ancient Israel*, London 1961, 346ff.

this particular cultic act, which appears to have been peculiar to Israelite practice,[47] is to be understood simply in terms of the requirement that the blood of sacrificial victims is to be devoted to Yahweh by pouring it out at the base of the altar or sprinkling it upon the altar (cf. Lev. 3:2, 8, 13; 7:2, 14; 9:18; 17:16; Num. 18:17; 2 Kgs. 16:13, 15). In view of this it cannot be maintained that the sprinkling of blood upon the altar signified the sprinkling of blood upon Yahweh thus creating a covenant relationship, as it is then interpreted, between him and Israel as the other partner in the rite.

Finally, apart from the blood rite, Exodus 24:3–8 also refers to a 'communion sacrifice'. Does this in itself provide evidence that the rite here described was a rite of covenant ratification? That this particular form of sacrifice would readily have lent itself to covenant-making ceremonies may well be the case. But this clearly does not mean that a 'communion sacrifice' was *ipso facto* a covenant sacrifice; nowhere in the Old Testament legislation concerning sacrifice is there any mention of a 'covenant sacrifice'. Accordingly, in the absence of other evidence one cannot simply argue that the 'communion sacrifice' mentioned in Exodus 24:3ff. was in itself a covenant-making sacrifice.

Thus far, therefore, we have seen that there are some grounds for believing the specifically covenant terminology in Exodus 19 and 24:3–8 to have been absent from the Sinai pericope in an earlier form and to be the work of a later, probably Deuteronomic, redactor who has worked over the earlier JE material in the pericope. Is this possibility contradicted by the presence of the covenant motif in Exodus 34?`

This chapter belongs to a larger complex comprising also chapters 32–3. The investigation of this complex is fraught with major difficulties and it is not my intention here to engage in a discussion of the many problems to which it gives rise. Most commentators ascribe the basic material in these chapters to J and E but acknowledge the presence of some Deuteronomic insertions and possibly also some P material. The dominating motif is the renewal of the covenant after the apostasy in making the gold calf. The record of this apostasy in chapter 32 as it now stands clearly presupposes the cultic enactments of Jeroboam I at the sanctuaries of Bethel and Dan (1 Kgs. 12)—a fact which poses a major difficulty for the

[47] On the significance of blood in Israelite sacrifice see D. J. McCarthy, 'The Symbolism of Blood and Sacrifice', *JBL* 88 (1969), 166–76.

view that the basic material in this chapter comes from the Yahwist who, as is now usually agreed, worked before the Disruption when Jeroboam I came to power in Northern Israel.[48] We need not concern ourselves further with this narrative, save only to observe that the apostasy of Jeroboam the son of Nebat is a particular obsession of the Deuteronomic authors, which might suggest that they had much more to do with shaping the final form of the narrative in Exodus 32 than is usually granted by commentators.[49]

Of more immediate importance for us is chapter 34 which centres on the renewal of the covenant after the apostasy recorded in Exodus 32. Once again, this chapter presents a number of problems, the most notorious being the description of the laws contained in the narrative as 'the ten commandments' (*v.* 28), there being apparently more than ten laws in the text as it now stands.

It has been argued by many scholars that these laws constitute a 'ritual decalogue' belonging to J as against the 'ethical decalogue' in Exodus 20 believed to belong to E. Recently, however, though not for the first time, it has been argued that the legal content of this chapter is a relatively late revision of the legislation contained in Exodus 23:14ff. with which it has long been recognized to be closely parallel. On the basis of various considerations, A. Phillips has contended that this revision was made in the light of Hezekiah's reformation in the late eighth century B.C. and he draws attention in particular to Exodus 34:23f., which appears to presuppose the centralization of the cult, adding that this may indeed be the distinctive development in Exodus 34:18ff.[50] Phillips believes this

---

[48] On the view that the basic material is E, it is argued by some that the original tradition constituted the *hieros logos* for the presence of a bull image as the pedestal of the invisibly present Yahweh at Bethel (cf. e.g. M. L. Newman, *The People of the Covenant*, New York–Nashville 1962, 181ff.). Noth suggests that the basic material may have been 'a subsequent literary addition to the J narrative which was inserted to accommodate the condemnation of the cult introduced by Jeroboam within the great comprehensive description of the pre-history and early history of Israel as provided by J' (*Exodus*, 246). But although the narrative as it now stands clearly presupposes the cultic policy of Jeroboam I, the possibility that the Yahwist himself, in the pre-Disruption period, engaged in polemic against the 'golden calf' in the cult at some shrines in Northern Israel is worth serious consideration (cf. G. W. Coats, *Rebellion in the Wilderness*, New York–Nashville 1968, 185f.).

[49] That the chapter embodies some Deuteronomic material (cf. esp. *vv.* 9–14 and see Noth, *Exodus*, 244) is widely acknowledged.

[50] A. Phillips, *Ancient Israel's Criminal Law*, Oxford 1971, 167ff.

revision to have been the work of the JE redactor working in
Judah after the fall of the Northern Kingdom. It seems to me more
likely, however, that those responsible for it were the Deuteronomic
authors: the centralization of the cult is a characteristic tenet of
their theology; we know that Hezekiah is the only king who, in
addition to Josiah, received unqualified praise from them in their
history; and besides, contrary to Phillips's view, it seems clear
that the material in Exodus 34:11–16 has a marked Deuteronomic
stamp.[51] But in any event, and of immediate importance for our
present purposes, it seems probable that the legislation in this
chapter, with which we must associate the reference to the making
of the covenant in *v.* 10 (cf. *v.* 28), derives from a relatively late
period in Israel's history. It only remains to conclude, therefore,
that the covenant motif in this chapter does not contradict our
conclusions arrived at earlier with regard to the absence of the
covenant terminology in the original JE material in the Sinai
pericope in Exodus 19:1–24:11.

To sum up: our examination of the Sinai tradition in Exodus
19ff. thus far has revealed the possibility that the belief in the
making of a covenant between Yahweh and Israel at Sinai emerged
and was incorporated into the Sinai tradition only at a secondary
and late stage in the development of this tradition.

In concluding this section of our study, however, it must be
stressed that these conclusions are advanced not as 'assured
results' but as a basis for further discussion. The foregoing
discussion is not an exhaustive investigation of all the problems
involved in determining the origin and history of the covenant
tradition itself in ancient Israel. It seems to me, however, that
the time has come to re-open the whole question of the origin of the
covenant, for I have found myself increasingly uneasy about the
way in which the covenant 'ideology' has been regarded more and
more as permeating almost every book of the Old Testament. In
particular and in spite of all the attempts to explain it, it surely
remains an enigma, if there was a covenant in early Israel, that the
very word for it, *berîth*, occurs only very rarely in the preaching of

[51] Phillips's statement (ibid., 169) that 'modern Pentateuchal criticism
has indicated that one should not expect to find the hand of the Deutero-
nomist in the Tetrateuch' is in the face of much evidence to the contrary.
On Exod. 34:11–16 see Noth, *Exodus*, 261ff.; J. P. Hyatt, *Exodus*, 324.
Cf. C. W. H. Brekelmans, 'Die sogenannten deuteronomischen Elemente
in Genesis bis Numeri. Ein Beitrag zur Vorgeschichte des Deuteronomiums', SVT 15 (Leiden 1966), esp. 94ff.

the pre-exilic prophets and that where it does occur (Hos. 6:7; 8:1) its originality in the text is subject to question. Furthermore, fresh consideration must surely be given to the fact that the very distribution of the word $b^e r\hat{\imath}th$ is concentrated to a pronounced degree in the Deuteronomic literature and literature which can be shown to be either dependent upon or at least influenced by it, as well as the widely acknowledged fact that the covenant between God and Israel receives its clearest formulation in Deuteronomy and related literature of the seventh and sixth centuries B.C. Furthermore, can we really accept the view, frequently advanced against the latter observation, that there was a covenant 'ideology' in the pre-Deuteronomic period but that it was understood in a different way from that in which the Deuteronomic authors understood it?[52] Did the Deuteronomic authors so alter the meaning of the word $b^e r\hat{\imath}th$ when applied to the Yahweh–Israel relationship that its usage in the literature which stems from them bears little resemblance to its usage before their time?

These and a number of other questions concerning the origin and history of the covenant in the Old Testament are currently being re-examined. For our present purposes, however, we need observe only that a question mark may plausibly be placed against the originality of the covenant motif in the Sinai tradition. We must therefore direct our attention now to the second major element of tradition in the Sinai narrative, namely, the theophany, Yahweh's awful manifestation of himself to Israel at mount Sinai. Was the theophany perhaps the original basis and content of the Sinai tradition, as some scholars have maintained?

III

Since the *locus classicus* of the theophany of Yahweh at Sinai is Exodus 19, we begin with a consideration of this chapter. The

[52] For example T. C. Vriezen, 'The Exegesis of Exodus xxiv 9–11', *OTS* 17 (1972), 117, n. 4 argues that Perlitt, who argues for the Deutero-nomic origin of the Covenant ideology in the Old Testament, 'too much has restricted his definition of "covenant", perhaps because he started his study of the covenant with the representation of it in the Deuteronomic theology, that has its own strongly marked idea of the covenant. Starting from this he thinks that the many older varying and different forms fall short of what in his opinion is the genuine idea.'

material here relevant for our discussion is contained in *vv*. 9–20. *Vv*. 1–2a derive from P; *vv*. 3b–8, as we have already observed, are probably from a Deuteronomic redactor and in any case are not concerned with the theophany, whilst *vv*. 21–25 are widely agreed to be a secondary addition to the material in *vv*. 9–20. The literary critical analysis of *vv*. 9–20 is a much disputed issue. Since, however, our primary concern is with the tradition preserved in this chapter we need not become involved in a discussion of the literary critical questions. For the sake of convenience, however, I have adopted Noth's analysis of the chapter.[53]

The J account narrates the instructions given by Yahweh to Moses for the preparation of the people for the theophany, the preparation itself and the ensuing theophany 'on the third' day. The holiness of the mountain is stressed and the penalty of death announced for anyone, except Moses, ascending or approaching it. When Yahweh 'descends' upon the peak of the mountain Moses alone is summoned to ascend. The presence of Yahweh on the mountain is described in terms of 'a thick cloud' of smoke, 'like the smoke of a kiln', and fire. *V*. 18 states that the mountain 'quaked greatly', though there is evidence for a reading which describes instead the people as trembling.

The E account, which is more fragmentary than the J material in this context, describes the theophany in terms of thunder and lightning and a 'dense cloud' upon the mountain. Moses leads the people from the camp to the foot of the mountain 'to meet God' and the trumpet blast, which 'grew ever louder' (this is not referred to in the J account), signifies the presence of God. There follows a conversation between God and Moses but we are told nothing of its contents. The response of the people is narrated in Exodus 20:18b–21, which is probably an E fragment and which many commentators believe to have belonged originally before the account of the Decalogue (Exod. 20:1–17) and to have followed immediately after 19:19 (E).[54] Here the terror-stricken people, fearing that if God continued to speak to them they would die, demand that Moses should henceforth communicate God's words to them, that is, act as mediator.

[53] M. Noth, *Exodus*, 151ff. To J belong *vv* 9–16a, 18, 20 (apart from a few minor glosses), whilst *vv*, 16a–17, 19 together with the fragment in *vv*. 2b–3a quite probably derive from E.

[54] Such a view begs the question whether the Decalogue is original here, but this need not concern us here.

We may note here that the description of the theophany at Sinai in the later Pentateuchal sources D and P is, as in J, also in terms of cloud upon the mountain and of fire (cf. Exod. 24:15–17 (P); Deut. 4:11f.; 5:23, 24; 9:15). The thunderstorm phenomena of the E fragment in Exodus 19:16 are not found in any of the other Pentateuchal descriptions of the theophany at Sinai.

Three important features of the descriptions of the theophany in Exodus 19 stand out:

(1) We note that in neither account is God actually seen; only the phenomena accompanying his presence at or on the mountain are described. This concealment of God in his theophany at the mountain is characteristic of the descriptions of the theophany in all the Pentateuchal sources: God himself is never seen. Even in the narrative of the theophany to Moses alone recorded in Exodus 33:18ff. (probably J) only Yahweh's 'back' is seen; 33:20 states that no man can see God and live. The only exception to this is the tradition in Exodus 24:9–11 to which we shall turn below.

(2) In both accounts of the theophany in Exodus 19 Moses plays an indispensable role as mediator between Yahweh and Israel; his presence here can in no way be regarded as secondary. The narratives afford no hint of an earlier stage of tradition in which Moses had no place or indeed even a less significant place.

(3) Finally, and closely connected with the latter, it seems clear that the theophany here is not presented simply for its own sake but in close association with the communication of God's will to Israel through Moses (cf. Exod. 19:9, 19; 20:18b–21): the theophany leads up to and is followed by proclamation.

In the light of these observations concerning the descriptions of the theophany in Exodus 19, we turn again to Exodus 24:9–11. We have already concluded that the tradition preserved in this passage is not to be understood as a description of the ratification of a covenant. It is not concerned with a rite but centres exclusively on Yahweh's theophany on the holy mountain. Indeed, what is here recorded is a theophany *par excellence*: it states in the most direct manner that the representatives of Israel on the mountain 'saw the God of Israel'; it describes what they saw beneath God's feet; it states that in spite of such an awful experience they remained unharmed[55] and then it states again that they saw God. It is this that forms the centre and bulk of the passage; it is upon this

---

[55] This is how we must understand the phrase 'but he did not stretch forth his hand against the leaders of Israel'.

remarkable theophany that all the emphasis is laid. Consequently, the importance attached by most commentators to the concluding phrase of this passage, 'they ate and drank', must be seriously questioned, for more often than not it has meant that the importance of the material preceding it has been neglected or at best underestimated. We have also seen that, in the absence of other indications that this passage is concerned with the making of a covenant, it is inadmissible to interpret the eating and drinking referred to at the end of it as having been a covenant meal. The activity of eating or eating and drinking before God is mentioned elsewhere in the Old Testament in contexts which cannot be understood in terms of covenant ratification (e.g. Exod. 32:6; Deut. 12:7; 14:26; 27:7; 1 Chron. 29:22).[56] There is no compelling reason for understanding the eating and drinking mentioned in Exodus 24:11 in a different way from the same cultic activity in such texts as these. This is surely a more direct and plausible interpretation of the activity in question than the understanding of it in terms of the making of a covenant concerning which there is not the slightest hint elsewhere in the passage.[57]

Let us now compare this description of Yahweh's theophany with the theophany tradition in Exodus 19. Firstly, the tradition in Exodus 24:9–11 says nothing of the phenomena described in Exodus 19; there is no mention of either cloud or thunderstorm, smoke or fire. In this respect it differs strikingly from the first feature of the theophany in chapter 19 noted above. It differs equally strikingly from the other features of the descriptions in that chapter. Thus, in chapter 19, great emphasis is placed upon Moses and his role as mediator between Israel and God. In Exodus 24:9–11, by contrast, no such emphasis is to be found. He appears here alongside others as apparently nothing more than one of the leaders of Israel and he sees nothing and does nothing that the others do not see and do. It cannot even be claimed that he is *primus inter pares* in this tradition, for although his name is mentioned alongside the anonymous seventy elders, other individuals are likewise mentioned.

---

[56] See also the comments on Exod. 18:1–12 above, 69f.

[57] The argument, that the overall context of the passage within the Sinai pericope renders the interpretation of this tradition in terms of covenant probable, cannot carry conviction. All the indications are that this short passage embodies an ancient tradition originally quite unrelated to the surrounding traditions in its present context.

Finally, and again in contrast to the tradition in chapter 19, in Exodus 24:9–11 neither Moses or any of the others with him says anything. Nor does God speak. Furthermore, the passage does not appear to anticipate any ensuing proclamation, as the narratives in Exodus 19 clearly do. In fact Exodus 24:9–11, save only for the absence of its original introduction,[58] is a unity in itself: it narrates the ascent of the mountain by the Israelite delegation, describes their momentous experience there and concludes with the statement 'they saw God and ate and drank'.

In view of these considerations it is clear that Exodus 24:9–11 embodies a tradition which is independent of the descriptions of the theophany in Exodus 19. Moreover, it is not only independent of them, it is almost certainly older. Thus the very fact that it states that God was seen by the representatives of Israel on the mountain is surely an indication that it is earlier than the tradition in chapter 19 and related texts in which the hiddenness of God is emphasized. In addition, the inconspicuous role of Moses in Exodus 24:9–11, compared with his dominant position in the narratives in Exodus 19 and elsewhere in the Sinai complex, evidences that the tradition in Exodus 24:9–11 is of greater antiquity than these other descriptions of the theophany at Sinai in which he stands unrivalled as the only one who can approach the nearer presence of Yahweh on the holy mountain.

But though the tradition in Exodus 24:9–11 is of greater antiquity than the tradition in chapter 19 and related texts concerning God's theophany at the holy mountain, the latter cannot be regarded as having been developed secondarily on the basis of the former. So little have they in common and so striking are the differences between them that such an understanding of the origin of the tradition in chapter 19 must be ruled out. In short, the tradition in chapter 19 is, like that embodied in Exodus 24:9–11, *sui generis*.

The importance of this for our present purposes is obvious, for it means that in discussing the relationship between the Exodus and Sinai traditions we must distinguish between the different Sinai traditions we have isolated in the Sinai pericope, the tradition

---

[58] *Vv.* 1–2 cannot have been the original introduction to *vv.* 9–11. *Vv.* 1–2 single out Moses as the one who alone is to draw near to God on the mountain, but the record of what took place in *vv.* 9–11 knows nothing of such a distinction between Moses and the others with him: they all alike share the same experience.

in Exodus 19 on the one hand and the more ancient theophany tradition in chapter 24:9–11 on the other.

Firstly, then, what conclusions may be drawn concerning the relationship between the Sinai tradition embodied in the JE narrative in Exodus 19 and the Exodus tradition? Here surely the evidence is that these traditions were interrelated from the beginning. For the figure of Moses which, as we have seen, was integral to the Exodus tradition from the beginning, is likewise integral to the tradition in Exodus 19 and cannot be regarded as having been only secondarily inserted or associated with it. There are no sound reasons—whether from a literary-critical, form-critical or traditio-historical point of view—for believing that the Sinai tradition embodied in the old JE narrative in Exodus 19 either originated or developed independently of the Exodus tradition in early Israel.

Secondly, what of the tradition in Exodus 24:9–11 which we have seen to be a more ancient tradition of the theophany than the tradition reflected in chapter 19? Here, too, Moses is mentioned and this might be taken as evidence that even the earliest Sinai tradition we possess presupposed the Exodus tradition. Here, however, the figure of Moses is at its weakest in the entire complex of Sinai narratives. His inconspicuous place is only heightened by the attempt of the redactor from whom *vv.* 1–2 derive to accord him a special role and privilege. Of such a role and privilege, however, *vv.* 9–11 know nothing. The Moses of *vv.* 1–2 is the Moses of the tradition in Exodus 19 and the Exodus tradition, that is, the unrivalled leader of Israel and the one who alone may approach the nearer presence of God on the holy mountain. In view of this it seems very likely tnat the tradition in 24:9–11 originated quite independently of the Exodus tradition and that the mention of Moses in it is secondary and arose when this ancient tradition was associated with the later Sinai tradition in Exodus 19 and related texts.[59] At an earlier stage this tradition mentioned only Nadab and Abihu and the seventy elders.[60]

Such a conclusion with regard to the tradition in Exodus 24:9–11 would appear on the face of it to support the view of von Rad and Noth that there was originally no connection between

---

[59] Noth, *ÜG*, p. 178 argues that Moses and Aaron were originally unmentioned in Exod. 24:9–11.

[60] Whether at a still earlier stage this tradition mentioned only the seventy elders, as Noth suggests (ibid., 178), need not concern us here.

the Exodus tradition and the earliest Sinai tradition. In reality, however, the independence of the tradition in Exodus 24:9–11 in its original form from the Exodus tradition need indicate nothing more than that it originated in the period *before* the Exodus. There are no sound reasons for ruling out such a possibility. For neither Israel nor the worship of Yahweh suddenly appeared on the scene in the ancient Near East. On the contrary, behind both there is a long and complex history and development, the ramifications of which we shall probably never uncover with any degree of certainty or detail. It is probable that Yahweh was worshipped in the pre-Exodus period and few today would deny that a community bearing the name Israel may have existed in the pre-Mosaic period and, further, that it may already have been a Yahweh-worshipping community. Given such possibilities, it is surely also possible that the two Sinai traditions which we have isolated in the Sinai pericope belong to separate stages in the history of early Israel, the one (Exod. 24:9–11) to the period before the Exodus and the other (Exod. 19 and related texts) to the period after it presupposing and developing alongside the Exodus traditions.

The question arises what gave rise to the ancient tradition in Exodus 24: 9–11. A short unit of tradition such as this can scarcely be expected to yield much information about its religio-historical background or its *Sitz im Leben* and consequently only conjectures as to its origin are possible. One such conjecture is that it arose as something in the nature of an aetiology explaining Israel's worship of Yahweh at his holy mountain. That is, it may have arisen as the *hieros logos* of the cult of Yahweh at Sinai, a cult-foundation legend of which there are a number of examples in the Pentateuch.[61]

As to the tradition embodied in the old JE material in Exodus 19 and related texts, it has, as many agree, a cultic stamp so that the possibility remains open that it was transmitted and developed within the context of a cultic festival in early Israel, though whether that festival was a covenant festival must be reinvestigated. At the same time the narrative element in this material should not be underestimated and the possibility must be allowed that stories of the momentous experiences of Israel's ancestors at Sinai after their escape from Egypt were in circulation from the earliest period.

[61] For a brief discussion see O. Eissfeldt, *The Old Testament: An Introduction*, E.T. by P. R. Ackroyd, Oxford 1965, 42ff.

One final question arises. If these observations and suggestions concerning the Exodus and Sinai traditions can be sustained, do they shed any light on the historical events behind the Pentateuchal narrative of Israel's Exodus from Egypt and her journey through the wilderness to Canaan? It cannot be too much stressed that so complex is the origin and history of the Exodus, wilderness and Sinai traditions that any attempt to reconstruct the historical events underlying them is at best tentative. Nevertheless, if there are no form-critical or traditio-historical reasons for doubting an original relationship between the Exodus tradition and the Sinai tradition embodied in Exodus 19 and related texts, it is possible that they preserve, however dimly, the memory of one and the same group of people who escaped from Egypt and later journeyed to Sinai. Furthermore, if the group who escaped from Egypt believed that their deliverance was miraculously brought about by Yahweh (we have seen that there are no sound reasons for doubting that Yahweh was associated with the Exodus from the outset), then it is surely all the more conceivable that they may have journeyed to the sacred mountain where he who had graciously delivered them was to be worshipped. In addition, since Moses appears to have been original to the Exodus tradition and to this later Sinai tradition and since also, as Noth himself maintains, he has a firm place in the theme of the preparation for the settlement in the land of Canaan, [62] it is surely plausible to see, if only in its barest outlines, a progression of the Exodus group not only from Egypt to Sinai but also subsequently to the borders of the promised land of Canaan.

[62] M. Noth, *ÜG*, 180ff.

Bibliography

Albright, W. F., 'The Names Shaddai and Abram', *JBL* 54 (1953), 173–204.

— 'The Song of Deborah in the Light of Archaeology', BASOR 62 (1936), 26–31.

J. M. Allegro, 'Uses of the Semitic demonstrative element Z in Hebrew', *VT* 5 (1955), 309–12.

Alt, A., 'The Origins of Israelite Law', *Essays on Old Testament History and Religion*, E.T. by R. A. Wilson, Oxford 1966, 81–132. (Originally published in German in 1934 and later in his *Kleine Schriften*, Munich 1953.)

Anderson, G. W., 'Israel: Amphictyony: 'AM; KĀHĀL: 'ĒDÂH', *Translating and Understanding the Old Testament* (Essays in Honor of H. G. May), ed. by H. Thomas Frank and W. L. Reed, New York–Nashville 1970, 135–51.

Andrew, M. E., *The Ten Commandments in Recent Research*, London 1967 (with J. J. Stamm).

Baentsch, B., *Exodus-Leviticus-Numeri*, Göttingen 1903.

Begrich, J., 'Berit. Ein Beitrag zur Erfassung einer alttestamentlichen Denkform', *ZAW* 60 (1944), 1–11 (now in his *Gesammelte Studien zum Alten Testament*, ed. W. Zimmerli, Munich 1964, 55–66).

Beyerlin, W., *Origins and History of the Oldest Sinaitic Traditions*, E.T. by S. Rudman, Oxford 1965. (German *Herkunft und Geschichte der ältesten Sinaitradition*, Tübingen 1961.)

— 'Die Paränese im Bundesbuch und ihre Herkunft', *Gottes Wort und Gottes Land*, Festschrift for H. W. Hertzberg, ed. by H. Graf Reventlow, Göttingen 1965, 9–29.

H. Birkeland, 'Hebrew *Zāe* and Arabic *Dū*', *StTh* 2 (1948), 201–2.

Brekelmans, C. H. W., 'Exodus xviii and the origins of Yahwism', *OTS* 10 (1954), 215–24.

Brekelmans, C. H. W., 'Het "historische Credo" van Israël', *TvT* 3 (1963), 1–11.

— 'Die sogenannten deuteronomischen Elemente in Genesis bis Numeri. Ein Beitrag zur Vorgeschichte des Deuteronomiums', SVT 15, Leiden 1966, 90–6.

Calderone, P. J., *Dynastic Oracle and Suzerainty Treaty*, *Logos* I, Manila, 1966.

Childs, B. S., 'Deuteronomic Formulae of the Exodus Traditions', *Hebräische Wortforschung*, Festschrift for W. Baumgartner, SVT 16, Leiden 1967, 30–9.

Clements, R. E., *God and Temple: The Idea of the Divine Presence in Ancient Israel*, Oxford 1965.

— *Abraham and David: Genesis 15 and its Meaning for Israelite Tradition*, London 1967.

Coats, G. W., 'The traditio-historical character of the Reed Sea motif', *VT* 17 (1967), 253–65.

— 'Despoiling the Egyptians', *VT* 18 (1968), 450–7.

— *Rebellion in the Wilderness*, New York–Nashville 1968.

Eissfeldt, O., *Die älttesten Traditionen Israels. Ein kritischer Bericht über C. A. Simpson's The Early Traditions of Israel*, BZAW 71, Berlin 1950.

— *The Old Testament: An Introduction*, E.T. by P. R. Ackroyd, Oxford 1965. (Translated from the third German edition of his *Einleitung in das Alte Testament*. Tübingen 1964.)

Fensham, F. C., 'Did a Treaty between the Israelites and the Kenites Exist?', BASOR 175 (1964), 51–4.

Fohrer, G., *Überlieferung und Geschichte des Exodus*, BZAW 91, Berlin 1964.

— 'Altes Testament—"Amphiktyonie" und "Bund"?', *Studien zur alttestamentliche Theologie und Geschichte*, BZAW 115, Berlin 1969, 84–119. (First published in *Theologische Literaturzeitung* 91 (1966) 801–16, 893–904.)

Gerstenberger, E., *Wesen und Herkunft des 'Apodiktischen Rechts'* WMANT 20, Neukirchen 1965.

Giveon, R., 'The Shosu of Egyptian Sources and the Exodus', *Fourth World Congress of Jewish Studies*, vol. I, Jerusalem 1967, 193–6.

Gressmann, H., *Mose und seine Zeit. Ein Kommentar zu den Mose-Sagen*, FRLANT 18, Göttingen 1913.

Helck, W., '*Tkw* und die Ramses-Stadt', *VT* 15 (1965), 35–48.

Herrmann, S., 'Der Name Jhw3 in den Inschriften von Soleb.

Prinzipielle Erwägungen', *Fourth World Congress of Jewish Studies*, vol. I, Jerusalem 1967, 213–16.

— 'Mose', *EvTh* 28 (1968), 301–28.

— *Israels Aufenhalt in Ägypten*, Stuttgarter Bibelstudien 40, Stuttgart 1970.

Hyatt, J. P., 'Were there an Ancient Historical Credo in Israel and an Independent Sinai Tradition?', *Translating and Understanding the Old Testament* (Essays in Honor of H. G. May), ed. by H. Thomas Frank and W. L. Reed, New York–Nashville 1970, 152–70.

— *Exodus* (New Century Bible), London 1971.

Jepsen, A., 'Berith. Ein Beigrag zur Theologie der Exilszeit', *Verbannung und Heimkehr*, Festschrift for W. Rudolph, Tübingen 1961, 161–80.

Korošec, V., *Hethitische Staatsverträge*, Leipzig 1931.

Kraus, H. -J., 'Gilgal: ein Beitrag zur Kultusgeschichte Israels', *VT* 1 (1951), 181–99.

— *Worship in Israel*, E.T. by G. Buswell, Oxford 1966. (German, *Gottesdienst in Israel*, Munich 1962.)

Kutsch, E., 'Gesetz und Gnade. Probleme des alttestamentlichen Bundesbegriffs', *ZAW* 79 (1967), 18–35.

— 'Der Begriff *berîth* in vordeuteronomischer Zeit', BZAW 105, Festschrift for L. Rost, Berlin 1967, 133–43.

— 'Von *berîth* zu "Bund"', *Kerygma und Dogma* 17 (1968), 159–82.

Lohfink, N., 'Zum "kleinen geschichtlichen Credo" Dtn. 26, 5–9', *Theologie und Philosophie* 46 (1971), 19–39.

McCarthy, D. J., *Treaty and Covenant: A Study in Form in the Ancient Oriental Documents and the Old Testament*, Analecta Biblica 21, Rome 1963.

— 'The Symbolism of Blood and Sacrifice', *JBL* 88 (1969), 166–76.

— *Old Testament Covenant: A Survey of Current Opinions* (Growing Points in Theology), Oxford 1972.

Mann, T. W., 'The Pillar of Cloud in the Reed Sea Narrative', *JBL* 90 (1971), 15–30.

May, H. G., 'Joshua', *Peake's Commentary on the Bible*, second edition by H. H. Rowley and M. Black, London and Edinburgh 1962, 289ff.

Mendenhall, G. E., 'Covenant Forms in Israelite Tradition', *BA* 17 (1954), 50–76.

— 'The Hebrew Conquest of Palestine', *BA* 25 (1962), 66–96.

Mowinckel, S., *Le Décalogue*, Paris 1927.

Newman, M. L., *The People of the Covenant*, New York–Nashville 1962.

Nielsen, E., *The Ten Commandments in New Perspective*, London 1968.

Noth, M., *Das System der zwölf Stämme Israels*, BWANT IV:1, Stuttgart 1930.

— *Überlieferungsgeschichte des Pentateuch*, Stuttgart 1948. (This work has now been translated into English by B. W. Anderson under the title *A History of Pentateuchal Traditions*, Englewood Cliffs, N. J., but came to me too late for references to it to be included in this book.)

— *Josua, Handbuch zum Alten Testament*, second edition, Tübingen, 1953.

— *The History of Israel*, revised English translation by P. R. Ackroyd, London 1960. (Translated from *Die Geschichte Israels*, third edition, Göttingen 1956.)

— *Exodus*, E.T. by J. S. Bowden, London 1962. (Translated from *Das zweite Buch Mose, Exodus* (Das Alte Testament Deutsch, 5) Göttingen 1959.)

— 'The Laws in the Pentateuch: Their Assumptions and Meaning', *The Laws in the Pentateuch and Other Essays*, E.T. by D. R. Ap-Thomas, Edinburgh and London 1966, 1–107. (Originally published in German in 1940 and later in his *Gesammelte Studien zum Alten Testament*, Munich 1960.)

Pedersen, J., 'Passahfest und Passahlegende', *ZAW* 52 (1934), 161–75.

— *Israel: Its Life and Culture*, *III–IV*, Oxford and Copenhagen 1940.

Perlitt, L., *Bundestheologie im Alten Testament*, WMANT 36, Neukirchen 1969.

Phillips, A., *Ancient Israel's Criminal Law*, Oxford 1970.

Porter, J. R. 'The Background of Joshua iii–v', *SEÅ* 36 (1971), 5–23.

Quell, G., Article on Covenant in G. Kittel, *Theological Dictionary of the New Testament*, vol. II, Grand Rapids 1964, 106ff. (first published in German in 1935.)

von Rad, G., *Old Testament Theology*, vol. I, E.T. by D. M. Stalker, Edinburgh and London 1962. (Translated from *Theologie des Alten Testaments*, I, Munich 1957.)

— 'The Form-Critical Problem of the Hexateuch', *The Problem of the Hexateuch and other Essays*, E.T. by E. W. Trueman Dicken, Edinburgh and London 1966, 1–78. (Originally published in German in 1938 and later in his *Gesammelte Studien zum Alten Testament*, Munich 1958.)

Redford, D. B., 'Exodus i 11', *VT* 13 (1963), 401–18.

Richter, W., 'Beobachtungen zur theologischen Systembildung in der alt. Literature anhand des "kleinen geschichtlichen Credo" ', *Wahrheit und Verkündigung*, Festschrift for M. Schmaus, Paderborn 1967, 191–5.

Rost, L., 'Das kleine geschichtliche Credo', *Das Kleine Credo und andere Studien zum Alten Testament*, Heidelberg 1965, pp. 11–25.

Schmidt, J. M., 'Erwägungen zum Verhaltnis von Auszugs- und Sinaitradition', *ZAW* 82 (1970), 1–31.

Sellin, E., *Geschichte des israelitische-jüdischen Volkes*, I, second edition, Leipzig 1935.

Simpson, C. A., *The Early Traditions of Israel*, Oxford 1948.

Smend, R., *Yahweh War and Tribal Confederation*, E.T. by M. G. Rogers, New York–Nashville, 1970. (Translated from *Jahvekrieg und Stammebund: Erwägungen zur ältesten Geschichte Israels*, FRLANT 84, Göttingen 1963.)

Smith, W. Robertson, *Lectures on the Religion of the Semites*, 3rd ed. by S. A. Cook, London 1927.

Stamm, J. J. See under M. E. Andrew.

de Vaux, R., *Ancient Israel: Its Life and Institutions*, E.T. by J. McHugh, London 1961. (Translated from *Les Institutions de l'Ancien Testament*, Paris, two volumes 1958–60.)

— *Histoire Ancienne D'Israël*, Paris 1971.

Vriezen, T. C., 'The Credo in the Old Testament', *Die ou Testamentiese Werkgemeenskap in Suid Afrika: Studies in the Psalms*, ed. by A. H. van Zyl, Potchefstrom 1963, 5–17.

— 'The Exegesis of Exodus xxiv 9–11', *OTS* 17 (1972), 100–33.

Weippert, M., *The Settlement of the Israelite Tribes in Palestine*, E.T. by J. D. Martin, London 1971. (Translated from *Die Landnahme der israelitischen Stämme in der neueren wissenschaftlichen Diskussion*, FRLANT 92, Göttingen 1967.)

Weiser, A., *Introduction to the Old Testament*, E.T. by D. M. Barton, London 1961. (Translated from the fourth edition of his *Einleitung in das Alte Testament*, Göttingen 1957.)

Wellhausen, J., *Prolegomena to the History of Israel*, E.T. by J. S. Black and A. Menzies, Edinburgh 1885.

Wildberger, H., *Jahwes Eigentumsvolk, Eine Studie zur Traditions-geschichte und des Erwählungsgedankens*, ATANT 37, Zurich 1960.

van der Woude, A. S., *Uittocht en Sinai*, Nijkerk 1961.

Index of Biblical References

Genesis
1–11 10
21:25ff 65
26:28ff 68
31:43ff 65, 68
34 14
49 12

Exodus
1–15 54, 55, 56, 58
1:11 54
3:18 35
3:21f 55
5:6–19 58ff
5:20 59
5:20ff 60
6:15 4
10:28f 56
11:2f 55
11–12 55
11–13 55
12:29ff 55
12:35f 55
14 55
14:5ff 55
14:15 54
15 34
15:22 5
15:22–5a 26
15:22—18:27 10, 26, 27, 62
15:23 5
15:24 5
15:25 5
15–18 46
16 26
16:35 46
17:1–7 5, 26, 27
17:6ff 5
17:7 5, 26
17:8ff 27
17–18 5
18 26
18:1–12 69f., 80

18:13–27 46
19 49, 50, 62, 74, 77ff, 80ff
19:1 7
19:1—24:11 5, 7, 27, 31, 43, 45, 47, 49, 52, 53, 61, 63, 76
19:3b–8 26, 29ff, 35, 50, 63
19:4 26, 50
19:5 64
19:7–8a 71
19:8 40
19:9 44, 79
19:10f 44
19:10–11a 43
19:12–13a 44
19:13b 43
19:14–15a 43
19:15b 43
19:16 43, 79
19:18 43
19:19 43, 78, 79
19:20–4 44
20:1 45
20:1—23:19 7, 49, 63
20:2 40, 44
20:2–17 44, 78
20:3ff 40
20:18 43
20:18b–21 44, 78, 79
20:22—23:19 50
23:13 9
23:14ff 75
23:16 8
23:20–33 7, 49, 50, 63
24:1–2 81, 82
24:1–11 7, 49, 50, 63, 67f
24:3–8 31, 44, 51, 69, 70ff
24:4 45
24:5ff 40
24:6 73
24:7 45
24:8a 73
24:9–11 6, 40, 43, 50, 68ff, 77, 79ff
24:11 69

Exodus—*cont.*
24:12 45
24:15–17 79
29:1 73
29:19ff 73
32 74, 75
32:6 80
32–3 74
32–4 5, 43, 45, 49, 61
33:9 43
33:10 43
33:18ff 79
33:19 43
33:20 79
34 74ff
34:3 44
34:5 43
34:5f 43
34:8 43
34:10 76
34:11–16 76
34:12 9
34:18ff 75
34:23f 75
34:24 44
34:27f 45
34:28 76

Leviticus
3:2 74
3:8 74
3:13 74
7:2 74
7:14 74
8:22ff 73
8:30 73
9:18 74
14:1ff 73
16:2 43
16:12 43
16:13 43
17:16 74
23:17 8, 9

Numbers
10–14 5
11:4 40
18:17 74
18:19 73
20:13 5
25:12 73
25:13 73
27:14 5
28:26 8
33 62

Deuteronomy
1:2 46
1:11 21
1:21 21
1:46 46
4:1 21
4:11ff 79
4:34 21
5–28 49
5:15 21
5:23 79
5:24 79
5:25 46
6:3 21
6:10ff 22, 23
6:20ff 3, 24, 25, 35
6:21–3 23
6:22 21
7:6 64
7:12ff 22, 23
7:19 21
8:7ff 22
8:11ff 22, 23
9:15 79
9:29 21
10:1–5 41
11:2 21
11:9 21
11:10ff 22, 23
11:13ff 22
12:7 80
13:2 21
13:3 21
14:2 64
14:26 80
21:1 21
26 8, 10, 33
26:2 22
26:5 20, 21
26:5b–9 2ff, 17, 20ff, 24, 30, 33, 34, 35
26:5b–10 22f, 24
26:6 20
26:7 20, 21
26:8 20, 21
26:9 21
26:10a 21
26:10b 22
26:15 21
26:18 64
27 7, 34
27:3 21
27:7 80
28 41

Deuteronomy—*cont.*
28:46 21
28:62 21
29:2 21
29:24 21
31:10–11 7
31:20 21
32:1 41
32:51 5
33:2 6, 18, 62
33:4 6
33:8 27
33:26 62
34:11 21

Joshua
2–6 28
3–4 9
3–5 28
4:23 28
5:6 21
9:16 9
10:6 9
10:9 9
10:15 9
14:6–14 9
18:2–10 9
18:3 21
18:9 9
18:10 9
24 7, 13, 24, 25, 26, 35, 41, 49
24:2b–13 3, 24f, 35
24:14ff 25, 35
24:14–15 14
24:19–24 25

Judges
2:21 21
5:4f 6, 18, 62
5:5 62
10:1–5 13
11:16f 46
12:7–15 13

1 Samuel
7:14f 35
12 4, 26, 34, 49
23:14ff 65
24:14ff 68

1 Kings
5:12 65
8:9 41
8:10 43

8:42 21
12 60, 74

2 Kings
16:13 74
16:15 74
17:36 21

1 Chronicles
29:10ff 22
29:14 22
29:22 80

Nehemiah
9 26
9:6ff 4

Psalms
44:2ff 34, 35
50 7
68:8–9 62
68:9 62
77:12ff 34
78 4, 26
78:2ff 34
81 7
81:6ff 35
95:8 27
97:10ff 35
105 4, 34
105:37 55
111:4 35
111:6f 35
132:12 66
135 4
136 4, 21, 34

Isaiah
1:2 41
6:4 43

Jeremiah
7:22 35
11:5 21
21:5 21
27:5 21
31:31ff 35
32:17 21
32:21 21
32:22 21

Ezekiel
20:6 21
20:15 21

Ezekiel—*cont.*
20:33 21
20:34 21

Hosea
2 22
12:1 65

Micah
6:1–2 41

Habakkuk
3:3ff 6, 18
3:3–4 62

Index of Authors

Albright, W. F. 62
Allegro, J. M. 62
Alt, A. 44
Anderson, G. W. 27
Andrew, M. E. 47, 52

Baentsch, B. 64
Begrich, J. 65
Beyerlin, W. 36, 42, 43ff, 47f, 51
Birkeland, H. 62
Brekelmans, C. H. W. 20, 21, 22, 69, 76

Calderone, P. J. 66
Childs, B. S. 21
Clements, R. E. 63, 66
Coats, G. W. 55f, 75

Eissfeldt, O. 28, 83

Fensham, F. C. 69
Fohrer, G. 52, 55

Gerstenberger, E. 47, 52
Giveon, R. 54
Gressmann, H. 4

Helck, W. 54
Herrmann, S. 54, 58
Hyatt, J. P. 20, 61

Jepsen, A. 65

Korošec, V. 37
Kraus, H.-J. 28
Kutsch, E. 65

Lohfink, N. 20, 21

McCarthy, D. J. 24, 25, 36, 47ff, 64, 65, 74

Mann, T. W. 62
May, H. G. 25
Mendenhall, G. E. 36ff, 44f, 46, 47f, 51
Mowinckel, S. 6, 44

Newman, M. L. 75
Nielsen, E. 47, 52
Noth, M. 1, 5, 7, 10, 11ff, 24, 25, 26, 27, 28, 30, 31, 35, 37, 40, 41, 55, 57ff, 62, 63, 68, 69, 71, 72, 75, 76, 78, 82, 84

Pedersen, J. 55
Perlitt, L. 70, 77
Phillips, A. 75f
Porter, J. R. 28

Quell, G. 64

von Rad, G. 1ff, 17, 18, 20ff, 28, 29, 30, 31, 32, 33ff, 44, 46, 53
Redford, D. B. 54
Richter, W. 20, 21
Rost, L. 20, 21

Schmidt, J. M. 27
Sellin, E. 7
Simpson, C. A. 28
Smend, R. 59, 60
Smith, W. Robertson 72
Stamm, J. J. 47, 52

de Vaux, R. 54, 56, 73
Vriezen, T. C. 22, 23, 25, 77

Weippert, M. 38
Weiser, A. 23, 26, 33ff. 43, 46
Wellhausen, J. 4, 37
Wildberger, H. 29ff
van der Woude, A. S. 22, 25